LIVING MISSION

HEARTBEAT    BREATH    MOVEMENT

THE AUTHORS:

MIRIAM SWAFFIELD:

Miriam Swaffield is the Student Mission Developer for Fusion, as an evangelist she is passionate every student feels equipped to share Jesus with their friends.

Miriam believes students can be spectacular, because their Creator still believes them to be so. Taking her whole life is an assurance to the integrity of her writing, may you experience the boldness of faith that she so freely shares.

Those willing to engage will unearth beneath the crafted eloquence and poetic language an undiscovered prophet. She is an affront to any vestige of mediocrity that might dissuade and distract us from our humanity.

Miriam has boundless energy and in her free time can be found making new friends, talking to puppies or uploading her latest dance video to YouTube.

RICH WILSON:

Rich Wilson is Team Leader for Fusion and believes unapologetically for a student movement. Having invested the last two decades of his life in local church he is convinced of its role in parenting student mission.

Rich is husband to Ness and the grateful father to two daughters. A contemplative Christ centred spiritually has formed in Rich an assurance of identity that extends beyond title and affirmation. It is from this place that we are incited to both acceptance and adventure.

Where opportunities present themselves Rich willingly exercises his appreciation for fine tasting food, imposes a somewhat eclectic musical persuasion and courageously defends his much-varied golfing exploits.

(Thanks to Harry Hogarth (Fusion Intern) for writing these bios – we would never have come up with this stuff!)

CONTENTS

INTRODUCTION

PART ONE: THE HEARTBEAT (RICH)

Fully focused
All play
Spiritual adventurers
Doing life together
See through lives
Growing pains

PART TWO: THE BREATH (MIRIAM)

Rosie's Student Linkup story
Andrew's fresher's week story
Darren's bag angels story
Miriam's college reps story
James's bike story
Tim's computer clinic story
Ashley's dartboard story
Ian's ultimate frisbee story
Josh and Naomi's cell alpha story
Gavin's housemates alpha story
Jacko's homeless alpha story
Anna's club mission story
Jane's empty cupboards story
Pippa and Miriam's last minute banquet story
Natasha's prayer and prophecy story
Ellie's international story

PART THREE: THE MOVEMENT (RICH)

What makes a great meeting?
What happens when you meet together?
How do you build community?
Discipleship pathways'

THE END OF THE BOOK AND THE START OF THE MOVEMENT (MIRIAM)

INTRODUCTION

This book is an invitation. An invitation to look again at a message that makes us alive as human beings and how we can spread it in a way that's natural, instinctive and fulfilling. Long before this digital age dawned, humanity had been hardwired for relationship with God. Programmed into our DNA is a living mission that, once activated changes how we view God, ourselves and the world around us.

When Jesus left the comfort of heaven and moved into a distinctly human neighbourhood, it wasn't an accident. There was no trapdoor to fall through or cosmic banana skin for Jesus to slip on that propelled him into human form. Out of committed community came a deliberate and intentional plan to reach out to humanity in a new way. Together the founders of sacrificial love paid the price so that we could be friends with God. The Trinity is the template for mission and community and we are made to live in their image.

Small groups of people, committed to one another and centred on Jesus transform the world.

This is living mission: small communities connected to, and part of, local churches moving into student neighbourhoods to show the student world what God is like. Fusion believes that these intentional communities can and must transform the student world. Indeed it has happened many times before in student mission history.

Down the years such communities have been called all sorts of things from holy clubs to cell groups to 'the order of a grain of mustard seed'. What is important is not the name or the format but the values they embody and express. For them to be intentional in reaching students they don't have to be made up solely of students, there just has to be a bias towards serving and loving this particular people group. Living missional community is the consequence of these values and this focus.

Fusion is committed to encouraging a new wave of cell groups, clusters and churches to be planted. We also want to inspire and breathe new life into existing small groups so the Church can reach the student world. This book is designed to do that and to cast a vision for what is possible, tell stories of what is happening and encourage a movement for the glory of God.

Miriam and Rich

PART ONE:

HEARTBEAT

WHAT IS THE HEARTBEAT?

Ever since Jesus first gathered his small band of disciples, missional communities have been pioneering the church forward. Structures and language have come and gone, methodology and expressions continue to morph and change, but the values that give them life have remained. These values are explored here under six headings:

1. Fully focused
2. All play
3. Spiritual adventurers
4. Doing life together
5. See through lives
6. Growing pains

These values are the heartbeat of missional communities. Jesus still calls us, calls students, just as he did his first disciples, into radical lives of intentional living together in community. When students hear this call and respond to the heartbeat of God for community - life, growth and mission are the overflow effect.

THE HEARTBEAT SUSTAINS LIFE

Your heart keeps you alive; it stops beating, so do you. It does its work in a hidden place, quietly (most of the time) pumping over 2.5 million litres of blood around your body each year. The heart is a muscle that never tires. The values we explore as part of missional communities have similar longevity.

After 2000 years they are still going strong and have sustained the life and growth of the Church. Like the life of God they are relentless and they form the foundation for following God.

THE HEARTBEAT CREATES RHYTHM

The heart creates a rhythm in which we live our lives. When we run around or exert ourselves physically the heart beats faster allowing us to sustain effort. When our bodies are at rest or asleep the heartbeat slows right down. Life organises itself around the heart and the inward values held there show up in our external lives. What we spend our money on, how we use our time and the quality of our relationships all point to the heart. Cultivating these six ancient values as the foundation for a community of disciples allows our beliefs to be enacted. When our behaviour is consistent with our beliefs we can live mission-shaped lives as part of a community and being intentional in this together helps us live it sustainably.

THE HEARTBEAT RESONATES OUT

If you put your ear or a stethoscope to someone's chest you will be able hear their heartbeat. If the heart is beating fast, a hand on the chest will be able to feel it pounding. Beyond the chest there are another twenty points in the body where the heartbeat can be detected. These pulse points signify that there is life and energy in the body. Our values are often hidden but the impact and outworking of them can be felt. These six values resonate with the life and agenda of Christ and ripple out through and beyond the missional community.

As you are intentional about your community, being inclusive and sharing Jesus with those yet to know him, the edges of your community become fluid and 'living water' flows out.

1. FULLY FOCUSED - JESUS CENTRED

'See now the power of truth; the same experiment which at first glance seemed to show one thing, when more carefully examined, assures us of the contrary.'
(Galileo Galilei)

When Jesus announces he is the way, the truth and the life, (John 14:6) his claim deserves more than a passing glance or a mild mannered response. We are taught not to stare from an early age, but Jesus is the exception: as individuals and a community, our gaze needs to be fully focused on him. In the busy-ness of university life, fixing our eyes on Jesus becomes an act of intentional seeking, rather than an assumption that, left unchecked, can fall out of sight in the midst of deadlines, nights out and thousands of people.

 CHANDELIERS AND GREAT DISCOVERIES

Galileo Galilei was born on 15 February 1564, he was the first born son of a famous composer and musician. At the age of seventeen while he was studying medicine at the University of Pisa his eyes were drawn to a swinging chandelier. When he compared its motion with his heartbeat, he noticed that the chandelier took the same amount of time to swing back and forth, no matter how far it was swinging. Galileo's curiosity continued to grow and led him to explore many more disciplines, most famously his love of astronomy.

One of the most sacred beliefs of Galileo's day was the Ptolemaic theory that the earth was the centre of the universe. Around the earth revolved the sun, moon, planets, and all the stars. Galileo began to put forth theories that contradicted long held beliefs about the anatomy of the universe. In 1609 an invention took place that meant there was no going back. That invention was the telescope and now there was a new lens through which to study the heavens and the earth.

This new lens would land Galileo in greater trouble, long held beliefs and theories didn't want to be challenged by new evidence. Previous generations of astronomers had been obliged to depend entirely upon the naked eye for making all observations. The telescope brought to light unsuspected possibilities, and laid bare the secrets that had eluded humanity since the earliest times. This new lens gave life new perspectives and resulted in greater wonder and marvel of the universe than was previously conceivable.

'What had before seemed only empty space was in reality filled with vast systems of worlds, which waited only the proper moment to reveal themselves in all their bewildering splendour'
(Henrietta Christian Wright)

The publication of a journal in 1632 on his theories and discoveries led to Galileo being summoned to Rome. The religious authorities couldn't stomach his findings that the earth moved at all, let alone orbited around the sun. Galileo was made to recant such heresy. It is rumoured that when he rose from his knees after signing the abjuration he stamped on the ground and whispered defiantly to one of his friends "It does move, though!"

AN AWKWARD ADJUSTMENT

Just as the earth moves around the sun, we are designed to live, move and have our being in relation to the Son. In choosing to follow Jesus we accept that we aren't at the centre of a universe in which everything revolves around our life. We choose to make adjustments and enter into God's way of living where we value a life centred on Christ. That adjustment often feels very painful and awkward as we become aware of how mistaken our thinking and actions have been and how misplaced our hopes and affections are.

When things are out of focus all sorts of mistakes can be made. Great theories, doctrines and philosophies can be built on misinformation. Our focus is affected by how we look at the world, what equipment we use and what our frame of reference is. We know in having that focus on Jesus we open ourselves to a dynamic truth that interacts with us and shapes our lives. We see in Jesus a way to the Father where, as well as gazing at God, we become aware of God's gaze on us.

A life that is centred on Jesus is transformed by him. It

becomes a signpost to heaven's agenda and demonstrates, when more carefully examined, deep truths about who we are and why we matter to God. A community that is centred on Jesus points to the very life of God. Members' love for one another declares to the watching world that they belong to God. Together they create a sound from heaven that resonates out to the people they meet, serve and live alongside.

Imagine the impact of a bunch of students in their accommodation block, choosing to intentionally live with the priority of pointing each other towards Jesus; loving each other as they learn how to navigate uni life; all the while being committed to their other mates who are yet to know God.

4D TRUTH

To be fully focused on Jesus is much more than a mental position, something that we have convinced ourselves of in our mind. To be fully focused on Jesus is about embracing Truth in a whole other dimension. When we read the gospels we encounter Jesus in 3D. He declared that he is the way, the truth and the life. To those early disciples this was a very relational truth.

Jesus talked, touched and hung out with them. A fourth dimension was also at work: the person of the Holy Spirit, convicting, healing, transforming and resonating life and truth (John 16:13). Not a vague and distant hope, but a hope that is an intimate and present reality. The Holy Spirit is the one who is representing Jesus in the midst of our community or Re-presenting Jesus. We can expect and anticipate Jesus being present with us through the Spirit as we focus on him. Missional communities are a place of encounter.

THREE DIMENSIONS OF JESUS

When we focus on Jesus, it could be said that we relate to him in three main ways. We see Jesus as friend, saviour and Lord.

"The Word became flesh and made his dwelling among us. We have seen his glory, the glory of the one and only Son, who came from the Father, full of grace and truth."
(John 1:14)

Jesus as our friend showed us how to live: humanity created in the image of God needed a lesson in living. Jesus modelled a life that pleased God and that related to all sections of society, all ages and all races. He demonstrated how highly prized and valued people are. He taught us how to live 4D lives in relation to the Spirit and with dependence on the Father. He came from a perfect community and modelled community with God's life and presence at the centre. He showed us what it looked like to be a friend of God and a friend of sinners. Jesus as our friend walks with us on campus, with our housemates, during our seminars.

"He was pierced for our transgressions, he was crushed for our iniquities; the punishment that brought us peace was on him, and by his wounds we are healed."
(Isaiah 53:5)

Jesus as our saviour removed every barrier to communion with God. On the cross he defeated the evil one, paid the price for our sin, identified with a suffering world and demonstrated sacrificial love. He made sure that we could not only be great friends with God but be one with God. The cross of Christ was the universe's greatest big bang and the ripple effect from Jesus as saviour is right relationships, with God and with one another. Boom! As people who have received forgiveness we can extend that to others. Living with right relationships not only dignifies our humanity, it allows us to be more fully human. Unforgiveness and sin distort who we are and how we see God, the world and one another. The cross is the lens by which we see and embrace the saviour. Jesus as our saviour gives us the freedom to love all those we encounter at university because we know we have first received an incredible gift of sacrificial love in Jesus.

"Therefore God exalted him to the highest place and gave him the name that is above every name, that at the name of Jesus every knee should bow, in heaven and on earth and under the earth, and every tongue acknowledge that Jesus Christ is Lord, to the glory of God the Father."
(Philippians 2:9-11)

Jesus as our Lord defeated death and rose from the dead. He is the risen Lord. The Lordship of Jesus means our lives are characterised by obedience and hope. We live to obey all that Jesus taught and lived; we obey not with blind faith, but with eyes wide open in gratitude that we should be co-workers with God. We live in sync with God's Kingdom rule to proclaim and demonstrate his way of life. We live lives of hope. Hope keeps us going and it reframes the present. In times of suffering, hardship and darkness, Jesus is present: 'Christ in us the hope of glory'. Nothing in life or death can separate us from the love of God. Our hope is built on a firm foundation, not an idea, but on a truth, a person, a deity who will never leave nor forsake us. Jesus as Lord transforms the way we approach uni life, modelling something entirely counter-cultural to the usual hedonistic, self-serving perspective of the student world.

While Jesus never asked his disciples for worship, neither did he stop or deflect the worship directed towards himself. When we are fully focused on Jesus and get to know him better, we can't help but worship him with our whole lives. Missional communities in their very presence and out-working, worship Jesus; this is the reason for their existence.

'Then the eleven disciples went to Galilee, to the mountain where Jesus had told them to go. When they saw him, they worshiped him; but some doubted.'
(Matt 28:16)

2. ALL PLAY – EVERYONE SERVES

'We ourselves feel that what we are doing is just a drop in the ocean. But the ocean would be less because of that missing drop.'
(Mother Teresa)

Our perspective about our contribution matters. It matters to God, it matters to ourselves and it matters to those who whose lives are enhanced because we play our part. Some see the 'drop' as insignificant, others recognise that without the 'drops' there would be no ocean. What Mother Teresa is saying, with all humility, is that our contribution really matters. When all play their part, oceans and rivers are created that bring life and hope. Indeed miracles can happen.

 MIRACLE OF DUNKIRK

In 1940, in the early part of World War II, the German forces were inflicting heavy casualties on the allied forces of Britain and France. As the German army swept across Europe, over 300,000 soldiers of the allied army were forced to retreat. Eventually they ran out of space and were trapped on a beach, against the English Channel in the small Belgian town of Dunkirk (Dutch for "Church in the dunes"). The German troops had the allied army completely surrounded and then proceeded to drop leaflets on the British forces telling them to surrender and that there was no hope of escape.

All of England knew the plight of these soldiers and were bracing themselves for the terrible news awaiting the fate of these men. His Majesty King George VI requested that Sunday 26 May 1940 be observed as a National Day of Prayer for deliverance at a time when Britain was staring military disaster in the face. Late in the night of May 25, a simple three word cryptic message was transmitted across the airwaves of England from the commander of the British Army at Dunkirk. The message was, "But-If-Not". The British people knew their Bible and they knew what those words meant. Like Shadrach, Meshach and Abednego in Daniel chapter 3 they were declaring to the world that they would not surrender but were calling on God to deliver them.

In a matter of hours, without obvious formal organisation, thousands of English citizens jumped in their private boats and began sailing across the English Channel towards the trapped troops. The boats were of every kind imaginable; from small fishing boats, trawlers, larger private boats, and even an Olympic racing yacht. At risk to their lives, many played their part and raced to the beaches of Dunkirk. As the nation's prayers were offered and acted out the British began an evacuation effort that lasted for nine days, during which the normally rough and unpredictable English Channel remained as smooth as a 'mill pond'. Yet, the day after the evacuation ended, 'the wind moved to the north, and giant breakers came rolling over the empty beaches'.

This extraordinary unfolding of events is what historians now call the "Miracle at Dunkirk".

LIES

The greatest feats are accomplished together, they are created by shared sacrifice and commitment and they create shared memories and stories. In an age of unparalleled individualism this story reminds us of our common humanity and that everyone has a part to play whether rowing a boat or kneeling in prayer, whether on the dance floor with our housemates, or outside the club handing out water to the queue.

In a culture where comparison with others is at epidemic levels, the temptation is to adopt a competitive posture and be the leading light, or to abstain from carrying any real responsibility and apathetically go with the flow. The lie is sugar-coated and shiny, it comes through our TV screens and mobile devices 24-7; it is believed all too readily. The lie attacks our core identity and taunts us: 'you have no intrinsic worth unless you have this, look like this, achieve this or you are as popular as this'. The lie taps into one of our deepest needs to be significant. Media and advertising have made sure that what the lie offers is out of reach. Those who are perceived to have made it soon realise they have bought into a massive lie. Individualism thrives on such lies, it puts 'me' back at the centre and the part I play is for my own gain.

SERVE OR DIE

Eleanor Roosevelt, the longest serving first lady in the history of the United States is quoted as saying "When you cease to make a contribution, you begin to die." Why does this ring true? Humanity was created intentionally to be intentional. Genesis chapter one declares that there was work for people to do. To not work or contribute is to deny the image of God we are called to bear. When we stop contributing or serving and we just live purely for ourselves, we begin to die. We become less human as we refuse to partake in the divine image and mandate.

God created us in his image (Gen. 1:26). That image was one of self-giving love, existing in community. It is because we bear the image of God that we are significant. We don't work to gain significance, we work and contribute because we are significant. Jesus knew he was significant, his Father affirmed him: 'This is my Son, I'm delighted with Him' (Luke 3:22). At this point Jesus hadn't even started his work. When he did start, he surrounded himself with people and commissioned them to play their part.

Some of the teachings of Jesus that had the most impact were actions that had to be explained later with words: none more so than when Jesus, fully aware of his own significance and identity, wrapped a towel around his waist and began to wash the disciples' feet (John 13:4). Jesus the servant-deity set an example for us to follow and in serving and playing our part we also discover our significance and true identity. Suddenly, our reason for being at university and studying for a degree does not revolve around our own gain, but locates us in a place and context from which to love others and be equipped to further serve.

ONE BODY, ONE MISSION

Imagine that every Christian student knew they were significant and that they had a part to play. Imagine that they were commissioned, trained and released to play that part. The universities and campuses would look different. Yes, they would be playing their part as they went about their daily lives, their study and friendships. However, that part becomes something that is amplified when students know they are playing it alongside others as part of an intentional committed community.

> *'An enormous eye or a gigantic hand wouldn't be a body, but a monster. What we have is one body with many parts, each its proper size and in its proper place.'*
> *(1 Cor. 12:19-10. The Message)*

In 1 Corinthians 12 Paul describes our connectedness to each other in outworking this commissioning. He describes a comical picture of the human body looking like one big eye or one big ear: uniformity so extreme that the church and mission just look ugly! The physical human body is beautiful and attractive, so is the Church and mission when, as part of a Christ- centred community, every part is released to be what it is created for.

Margaret Mead famously said "Never doubt that a small

group of committed people can change the world. Indeed, it is the only thing that ever has." Without God this is possible but, with Christ at the centre, this change affects spiritual destinies as well. Paul is urging the church to work together, to value each other and the different gifting and contribution each of us brings. This part of the bible is very clear that we all have a part to play and we need each other to play our part effectively. Your story of living for Jesus at university is a vital component in the stories of other Christians around you and the life of the local church. You were not made to go it alone.

3. SPIRITUAL ADVENTURERS – DISCIPLESHIP

'People travel to wonder at the height of mountains, at the huge waves of the sea, at the long courses of rivers, at the vast compass of the ocean, at the circular motion of the stars; and they pass by themselves without wondering.'
(St. Augustine)

When we think about discipleship, we think about our whole lives. There is no part of our activity and being that isn't impacted by the call to follow Christ. That call to follow leads us into an adventure; one where we can stare in wide-eyed wonder at the creation all around us and also, one that is all about us. Relationship with the God of creation becomes the ultimate adventure, from which all other adventures have a point of reference.

 WILL YOU HELP ON THE WILD WAVES?

Legend has it that brightly lit angels hovered over the house when St Brendan was born in Annagh, Co. Kerry in 484. He was schooled in a monastic environment from a young age and was baptised and ordained a priest by Bishop Erc in 512.

St. Brendan was known as Brendan the Voyager or Brendan the Navigator. Of all the Irish saints, St. Brendan was the most adventurous. He belonged to that glorious period in the history of Ireland where great tales and legends were conceived. The birthing of Christianity for this island was taking place and they were commissioning their earliest messengers of the faith to unfamiliar lands and seas. The stories of St. Brendan voyaging over perilous waters were popular in the Middle Ages and continue to thrill and inspire today.

St. Brendan set up a lot of monasteries in Ireland. The one at Ardfert, at the foot of Mount Brandan in Co. Kerry is the most well known. It was from here that he set out on his most famous voyage. On the Kerry coast, he built a coracle of willow, covered it with animal hides, set up a mast and a sail, and after a prayer upon the shore, embarked in the name of the Trinity. A manuscript written in the 9th century tells of his journeys. It is thought he probably travelled to Iceland, Greenland and maybe even America. The manuscript is full of the adventures of his journey. One story tells how St. Brendan landed on an island that was actually a great big sea-monster. Another story tells how he narrowly escaped a sea-cat as big as a horse!

Wrapped up in the myths and legends of St. Brendan we discover some deep truths. Not least that the discipleship journey is one of great adventure. The prayer attributed to him below captures the heartbeat and passion we are exploring.

ST. BRENDAN'S PRAYER

Shall I abandon, O King of mysteries, the soft comforts of home? Shall I turn my back on my native land, and turn my face towards the sea?

Shall I put myself wholly at Your mercy, without silver, without a horse, without fame, without honour? Shall I throw myself wholly upon You, without sword or shield, without food and drink, without a bed to lie on?

Shall I say farewell to my beautiful land, placing myself under Your yoke?

Shall I pour out my heart to You, confessing my manifold sins and begging forgiveness, tears streaming down my cheeks? Shall I leave the prints of my knees on the sandy beach, a record of my final prayer in my native land?

Shall I then suffer every kind of wound that the sea can inflict? Shall I take my tiny boat across the wide sparkling ocean? O King of the Glorious Heaven, shall I go of my own choice upon the sea?

O Christ, will You help on the wild waves?

DISCIPLESHIP JOURNEY

Humanity is wired for adventure, we are naturally inquisitive and curious. It is easy to get caught up with the wonder of creation and a desire to explore the world out there. That is something we are designed to do. The outward adventure is designed to mirror the inward adventure, just as demanding but much more hidden. The inward adventure is about being centred on Christ and is a divinely inspired transformative journey. We call that inward adventure 'discipleship'.

I am convinced discipleship is most transformative when surrounded by wild waves. The waves come in different forms such as disappointment, uncertainty, grief and fear. They arise from situations that lead us to feel that our lives and emotions are out of control. We desperately want the waves to calm down, for the situation to change, to regain control and for the suffering to stop. However, discipleship is rightly called an adventure: we must endure many highs and lows in life and by doing so have a story worth telling.

WHAT IS THE DESTINATION?

If we are on a journey, what is the destination? To invest our lives in such a costly journey we need to know the destination is worth it, otherwise why bother? The great thing about this journey is that we get to taste the destination here and now. The destination could be described as an ever-deepening awareness of the love God has for us; a love from which we can't be separated by life or death; a love that is found in relationship and that sustains us on the wild waves.

Discipleship means that we take our lead and values intentionally from Christ. The alternative is to be influenced and led by the people we spend time with and listen to, whether they are physically present or on our TV screens. It is clear that Christians in their teens and twenties are more discipled by media and advertising than by scripture (God's truth). This isn't surprising as the majority of our time is spent under a power shower of advertising. Couple this with spending years sitting in lecture theatres being preached to and we find that our life-orientation needs to be intentionally brought back into alignment with God's truth. The good news is that truth is much more compelling and a short time spent getting our bearings in scripture each day can help us navigate through. The regular rhythm of meeting in missional community is also essential for keeping our discipleship journey on track through university.

4. 'SEE THROUGH LIVES' - LIFESTYLE

'I did not know I was on a search for passionate aliveness. I only knew I was lonely and lost and that something was drawing me deeper beneath the surface of my life in search of meaning. There is a hunger in people to go to those deep depths; to know that our lives are sacred; that our hearts are truly capable of love. It is a yearning to be all that we can be. A longing for what is real.'
(Anne Hillman)

One of humanity's deepest needs is to know and be known. When people get to know the real me and accept me and enjoy my presence, I have arrived at a place of tremendous freedom. I feel understood, validated and affirmed. I feel passionately alive. However, in order to know others at a deep level, I have to be prepared to make myself vulnerable. My freedom is connected to my vulnerability.

 THE CAGE OF FREEDOM

'God gave me a vision of myself in a cage, with a mate, outside York Minster'. That was the catalyst for what would become an exciting and challenging week for Luke Smith and his second year student friend Gavin. A cage 8ft x 4ft in size was erected outside York Minster and for 168 hours Luke and Gavin stood in there, sat in there, went to the toilet in there and slept in there – for a whole week. They called it the 'Cage of Freedom'.

Taking inspiration from St Paul who said, "Though I am free and belong to no one, I have made myself a slave to everyone, to win as many as possible" (1 Cor 9: 19). They set out to imprison themselves for a week. They took only a bottle of water into the cage with them and trusted that God would provide for their needs and would keep them safe as they faced their fears and exposure.

As the week went on Luke and Gavin spoke to over two thousand people about Jesus, about his love for people and about the freedom he offers people when they feel trapped. The impact was amazing. They had to contend with all sorts of responses and at times ridicule from drunks, to stag do's, to well-dressed businessmen. They had clear answers to their own prayers for provision, protection and peace.

They also had the privilege of praying for over 50 people and leading 3 people to Christ. People came and brought them so much food that they had to give 90% of it away. Luke explained 'The vast majority was given by complete strangers who came over and chatted to us. Some people would love what we were doing and others would hate it, but they still brought food back for us.'

By trapping themselves in a cage Luke and Gavin made themselves vulnerable and put the power in the hands of those on the outside. This made people feel safe, so they

> felt that they could come and ask them what they were doing and walk away when they chose. They discovered that God just kept bringing people who needed to experience his peace and freedom.

A VULNERABLE DEITY

By giving up his divine privileges and becoming a naked human baby, Jesus embraced a level of vulnerability that is difficult to comprehend. At the same time, so also did God the Father, as Jesus was going to reveal his nature like never before. That vulnerability would eventually lead to the cross and a moment of surrender, so that we can all know and be known by God. For the first time the world could 'see' God and he was not what people were expecting.

The lifestyle and values of God were now on display. Jesus was very deliberately living a 'see through life'. His disciples' pleaded 'show us the Father' and Jesus replied, 'Anyone who has seen me has seen the Father' (John 14:9). Unlike us, God wasn't afraid to show us who he really is, what he is really like. God carries not the slightest bit of shame and makes no apology for his image. He has no self-esteem or comparison issues, God is the template and he desires to be vulnerable and transparent with his identity.

PLEASE COME IN

The door of my house remains most of the time firmly shut

and locked. If someone comes to my door and I don't know them, I open the door cautiously. I don't find it easy to let people I don't know into my home and my life. It seems God is not like me! His front door doesn't have a lock, it doesn't even seem to have a door, just a way in. There is sign saying 'please come in' and 'make yourself at home'. Jesus lived an open and transparent lifestyle that allowed all people in.

He journeyed intentionally in community with his disciples and they got the greatest insight into his life and values. They witnessed the most unlikely people-connections and conversations. They participated in events which, for their culture, were hugely inappropriate, but for God they were sacred. A woman by a well (John 4), men with skin diseases (Matt. 8), children (Matt. 19), prostitutes (Matt. 21:31) and blind beggars (Mark 10:46) were some of the unlikely people allowed in. Jesus laughed and wept with his disciples, he even let them in on very personal moments like the transfiguration and the garden of Gethsemane.

ACCOUNTABILITY

Missional communities can only be effective if they are authentic and the message is consistent with the medium. Fortunately God has not only demonstrated to us how to live 'see-through lives', he has given us each other to be accountable to. Accountability is a gift that works for our benefit on lots of levels. In James chapter 5 we are urged to 'confess our sins to one another'. This might seem strange when it is God who ultimately forgives us our sins. We are forgiven, but in order to be free we often need the help of others. Through making ourselves vulnerable by confessing our struggles and weaknesses, we find new strength and freedom.

Through confession and accountability we confront our hidden life and secret sin and are freed to live more authentically without fear of exposure and rejection. It is impossible to be passionately alive whilst battling shame and condemnation. Having experienced God's reckless inclusivity and other people's kindness in accepting us, we are in a more courageous and compassionate place to accept others. Accountability frees us to go deeper in all our relationships. It frees us to love and serve as Jesus loved and served.

When a small group of students gather in a room together, there is less space to hide. When twos and threes from this group commit to asking each other the uncomfortable questions that probe deeper into how they are following Jesus and wrestle through the stumbling blocks along this journey, new levels of discipleship and maturity in faith result.

MISSION-SHAPED LIVES

Individual 'see-through lives' make an impact; a community where this lifestyle is the norm shows the world that this group of people belong to God. Jesus declared to his disciples that 'by your love for one another the world will know that you are my disciples' (John 13:35). 'See-through lives' that allow the life and light of Christ to shine are naturally mission-shaped lives. Mission is a consequence: our lives, love and service provoke curiosity and we must be ready to give an answer for the hope we have (1 Peter 3:15).

When Fusion first started, one of the most common answers to the question of why students became Christians was because they saw something in the community of Christians who were part of cell groups. Students from un-churched backgrounds would remark that they had never seen this quality of relationship and depth of love for others. They could see it and they wanted in. It is time once again to be intentional in creating and living in missional community as students, the consequence of which will be more students meeting and following Jesus.

5. DOING LIFE TOGETHER - COMMUNITY

'And I'd join the movement,
If there was one I could believe in
Yeah I'd break bread and wine,
If there was a church I could receive in
'Cause I need it now'
(U2, Acrobat Lyrics)

There is a deep longing and yearning inside each one of us to be part of something bigger than ourselves: something that makes a difference and that causes us to lift our heads away from the immediate highs and lows; something that distracts us from our own selfish ambition; something that is real, that gives life and that we can be part of.

 OPEN HEAVEN STORY

When I (Rich) was a student I got caught up in the smallest of movements. It didn't look like a movement from the outside but on the inside it was a God-charged space where no dream seemed too ridiculous. It started when seven recent graduates from Loughborough University decided to stay living in the town and plant a church with a clear focus on reaching and building community among students.

This group of people all lived in the same house and

modelled doing life together. They called themselves Open Heaven as they aspired to make the goodness of heaven available to the town and students and to see the will of God done on earth as in heaven. Right from day one there was a strong emphasis on right relationships, discipleship and values of openness, honesty and accountability. This was the foundation for what would become a strong and vibrant community, committed to God and each other.

Before long there were numerous community households doing life together and a network of missional cell groups seeking to include others in this community. Like all human and spiritual communities it didn't get built without challenges and there have been set-backs, disappointments and tragedies along the way. I discovered that when Jesus is at the centre those hard times became the furnace for transformation and greater fruitfulness.

Without entering into the spirit of the age and being competitive around growth and numbers we still want to boast of what God has done with us and in us. We have done our best to reach students and over the last 20 years have seen around 1000 students be part of one-to-one discipleship, trained as leaders and given responsibility. Around 25% hadn't made commitments to follow Jesus until they joined the community and the majority have been sent on from Loughborough as we have commissioned them to make a difference in their future workplaces and other church communities.

Many others have stayed around to commit to building Open Heaven and work for the transformation of Loughborough and seek peace and prosperity for the town. Businesses, charities and projects have been set up to create employment, generate wealth and alleviate poverty. Singles, marrieds and children are creating shared households and modelling extended family. We are aspiring to bring a little bit more of heaven to earth.

We are continuing to do life together, love students and the story continues....

MAKING MEMORIES

Peter had given up; that moment around the fire when the cockerel crowed showed him that he didn't have what it takes. It was a vivid and painful memory that clung to him like the smoke from the fire on his clothing. Now he was back in the boat doing what he knew he could do. Then two things happened that would evoke memories and affirm his destiny.

In John 21 Jesus instructed the disciples to let the nets down again after a fruitless night's fishing. The haul of fish was so great they couldn't pull the nets in. What was going on? Around three years earlier in Luke 5 this 'haul of fish' was a sign for Peter that he was to be part of a much bigger movement. Had he forgotten? This was a reminder designed to cement that memory and the call to follow Jesus.

Peter was ecstatic, he was being called again and he jumped in the water to be with Jesus. When he reached the shore the smell of smoke from the fire greeted him and his whole body shuddered. In an instant he was back around 'that' fire, his stomach in knots and this unresolved memory haunting him.

"Our sense of smell is 10,000 times more sensitive than any other of our senses and recognition of smell is immediate. Other senses like touch and taste must travel through the body via neurons and the spinal cord before reaching the brain whereas the olfactory response is immediate, extending directly to the brain. This is the only place where our central nervous system is directly exposed to the environment."
(von Have, Serene Aromatherapy)

This is Jesus at his redemptive best, and I think he creates this whole environment especially for Peter. With the smell of smoke in the air and the associated memory of failure, he starts a conversation with Peter to create a new memory. Three commissions now replace three denials and Peter knows that he has been forgiven.

LIFE IS MESSY

We all mess up, make mistakes and sin. The great news is that if we desire to continue to follow after Jesus these things don't disqualify us, but they do impact on our relationships. Doing life together is messy and when our mess causes pain to ourselves and others we need to find ways of making new memories.

Commitment to God and each other means we don't just up and leave but find ways to heal and restore relationships. Broken relationships are the root cause of poverty and pain. In doing life together we need to be able to confront and correct one another and be able to give and receive forgiveness.

Making friends becomes the number one priority at the start of university life, but finding authentic and committed relationships is a very different matter. From Freshers' week, the pattern for students connecting relationally forms around the three basic questions of "what's your name?", "where do you come from?" and "what are you studying?" Many friendships are formed over initial nights out, in a mixture of nervousness, alcohol and a pressure to find and connect with people. Student friendships can be swapped, changed, moved-in or moved-out, so missional communities of students living in vulnerable commitment to each other as family, not just fair-weather friends, speak of something very different.

We need to have the courage to enter into conversations that we would rather not have, in order to be faithful to one another as we model Christ-like relationship. The outcome of such open and honest relationships is that people feel loved and valued and that a depth of relationship is cultivated that reflects the heart of God in community.

BUILDING TOGETHER

"In Luke's Gospel, Jesus is either going to a meal, at a meal, or coming from a meal," says Robert Karris. It seems the primary means by which Jesus built community, made disciples and lived a mission-shaped life involved food. In Luke 7 Jesus announced: "The Son of Man has come eating and drinking, and you say, 'Look at him! A glutton and a drunkard, a friend of tax collectors and sinners!'"

Eating and drinking are the building blocks of our lives and are what we have in common with every person on the planet. This common ground is more than just a survival mechanism, it is the basis of our deep need, to know and be known, being met. Through eating and drinking, with values of hospitality and generosity, we cultivate deep, committed relationships and build missional community together.

In student halls of residence everyone misses sitting on sofas and mum's home cooked food. Uni housing doesn't feel like home when you're wearing three jumpers to save on heating bills. In these new homes, missional communities become the answer to the desire for family and hospitality in the student world. Being generous in cooking for all your course mates and friends is inclusive of everybody and creates a different culture when students on a budget and limited cooking experience usually cater for themselves alone.

6. GROWING PAINS - MISSION, MULTIPLICATION AND MOVEMENT

'My gracious Master and my God,
Assist me to proclaim,
To spread through all the earth abroad
The honours of Thy name.'
(Charles Wesley)

It is reassuring to partner with God in building and establishing a movement, the success of which he is committed to. Ours is a contribution of faith: much of what we serve and sacrifice for is hidden below the surface. Faith then is a conviction that we know that God sees and directs what is going on. In him all things hold together and God rewards faithfulness not results. John Wesley had his eyes on Christ and was unaware a revival was happening around him.

 THE HOLY CLUB

Nearly 300 years ago in Oxford University a small group of students were attempting to live differently and it was being noticed. This was a group of students who were concerned about their souls and about a relationship with God, if that was possible. They met together to study and reflect on Scripture. They set aside time to pray and fast, gave themselves to good works, visited those in prison and provided food for poor families. Their lives appeared overly ordered and odd to those looking on.

The rest of the university held them in total contempt. The Holy Club was the name given to John and Charles Wesley's group by their fellow students in mockery of their emphasis on devotions. They were derided and called Methodists because of the method by which they lived their lives. John Wesley's zeal took him on mission to North America where he came face to face with his own limitations, burnout and failure.

That might have been that, had it not been for a meeting with Peter Bohler a Moravian missionary. Wesley spent much of his spare time with Bohler losing arguments (most notably conceding that salvation is by faith not works). In May 1738 Wesley wrote in his journal this account of a meeting Peter Bohler had invited him to.

'In the evening I went very unwillingly to a society in Aldersgate Street, where one was reading Luther's preface to the Epistle to the Romans. About a quarter before nine, while the leader was describing the change which God works in the heart through faith in Christ, I felt my heart strangely warmed. I felt I did trust in Christ alone for salvation; and an assurance was given me that He had taken away my sins, even mine, and saved me from the law of sin and death.'

This meeting has become known as Wesley's Aldersgate experience and this new found fire would also consume the Holy Club. The Holy Club never exceeded 25 members, but would see many go on to be revivalists.

> John Wesley became a familiar figure on horseback and travelled 250,000 miles in his lifetime. He preached 40,000 sermons to crowds sometimes of over 20,000 and raised up 10,000 society and band leaders (missional small group leaders).
>
> Charles Wesley became a prominent English hymn writer, poet, and preacher who wrote over 5,500 hymns including "And Can It Be That I Should Gain?", "O for a Thousand Tongues to Sing", and "Hark! The Herald Angels Sing". The impact and legacy of this small group continues to serve and inspire many around the world today. And it all started when they were at university.

STRANGELY WARMED

The Holy Spirit makes the difference to mission. The imagery in Acts 2 of the Holy Spirit is that of hurricane strength winds and wild fire. The Holy Spirit, like these elements of nature, is not domesticated and subject to human control. It is our responsibility, by faith, to place ourselves in the slipstream of the Holy Spirit and seek out and celebrate the life of God wherever it touches earth. When the heart is 'strangely warmed' by the Holy Spirit it adds a new dimension of power to mission.

I am convinced the first manifestation of the Holy Spirit at work in us is a release of boldness and courage. For Peter in Acts 2, that led him to preach to a crowd of 3000, for others it led to great acts of generosity in sharing possessions and giving away money. In Acts 4 the apostles prayed for more boldness and the Holy Spirit filled them:

> *'And now, O Lord, hear their threats, and give us,*
> *your servants, great boldness in preaching your*
> *word. Stretch out your hand with healing power; may*
> *miraculous signs and wonders be done through the*
> *name of your holy servant Jesus.'*

After this prayer, the meeting place shook, and they were all filled with the Holy Spirit. Then they preached the word of God with boldness.

GROWING PAINS

In our culture we love the story and the end result. We like the cultivation of the story less, especially if it involves some suffering, pain and sacrifice. The best stories and the most celebrated achievements have the greatest cost. Growing pains are common through pregnancy and childhood and they are necessary for new life and maturity.

In raising up disciples, Jesus had the joy of their company and enthusiasm and also the pain of their mistakes, doubts, denial and betrayal. If we want to grow and multiply groups of disciples, we will have growing pains. I remember many occasions being part of a growing small group and cultivating fantastic depth of relationship and community. A few people made commitments to Christ for the first time and others were growing in their faith. It would have been easy to stop there and put a sign up effectively saying 'church full'.

Cosy community is not what the wild Spirit has in mind. It is okay for a season to get healed and restored but God has mission and maturity in his sight. Multiplication is needed for the movement and we must allow God's eternally new life to be breathed into us. For me that has meant taking some deep breaths before sharing the vision for why we must sacrifice this community in order for more people to be part of it.

Multiplication has cost. When being a Christian student places you in the minority amongst your peers, the temptation is to hold on to the little community you have established, where you are secure and understood, is powerful. But we must keep challenging ourselves not to sit comfortably in our own Christian bubble. The strong relationships continue and are celebrated in larger church gatherings. In multiplying a small group community, space for new relationships to form is created. I have found that once a small group hits double figures, if it didn't multiply, then the relationships wouldn't go as deep, as there was less space to hear and be heard. Commissioning two new missional communities from the original one meant we remained radically inclusive and expectant of new life. This side of heaven the church is never full.

MOVEMENT

Movement is the result of mission and multiplication. Jesus breathed on his disciples and that breath continues to give life and purpose to the Church. Jesus somewhat recklessly commissioned a group of young men to continue his work of proclaiming and demonstrating the Kingdom. God is a risk taker. He risked leaving the cosy community in heaven to come to earth. He risked pain, separation and sacrifice on the cross and he risked leaving the work in the hands of disciples who only recently had deserted him.

Risky and reckless, but trusted to the Spirit. The Spirit fires up the movement and provides the boldness and courage to keep giving ourselves away and to keep making space for new people in our lives. Jesus modelled missional community that embraces growing pains and he is asking you to follow him in the same way.

'We are not now that strength which in old days
Moved earth and heaven; that which we are, we are;
One equal temper of heroic hearts,
Made weak by time and fate, but strong in will
To strive, to seek, to find, and not to yield.'
(Alfred, Lord Tennyson)

PART TWO:

BREATH

WHAT IS THE BREATH?

If a body doesn't breathe, it doesn't live. The lungs spend their time inhaling oxygen, which the blood needs to sustain the body and keep the heart pumping. They then release that which the body does not need as they exhale. This constant exchange with the outside world that occurs with our every breath is vital to life, growth and health. A missional community needs constant inhalation from outside itself: breathing in new life, inspiration, energy and people to refuel, revitalise and renew the body; then breathing out again with power and impact. Genesis 2 describes: 'Then the Lord God formed a man from the dust of the ground and breathed into his nostrils the breath of life, and the man became a living being.' The breath is the life of God, in us, in the church, and to the world yet to know this good news.

THE BREATH ENABLES ACTION

Just as the heart needs the body to take exercise in order to remain healthy, so missional community is sustained by movement and activity. The body without exercise is in trouble... faith to without deeds is dead. However, keeping active is not just for internal benefit in order to pump the same blood around the same body. As we exercise and move, our lungs work harder and more efficiently, breathing-in and giving-out in equal measure. The church is not here to maintain itself and keep its existing members comfortable in an inward health-cycle. Refreshing, renewal and release are occurring in a constant exchange. As we are active in our faith and sharing Jesus, passing on what we have received, new life is created. Mission is a natural product of a healthy, active community, and a climate of change becomes the predominant culture.

The breath of life enables action.

BREATH BRINGS GROWTH

Out of life, comes more life. When you begin regular exercise, your lung capacity increases as your body is trained to sustain itself, pushing to run further and faster, lift heavier weights, react more quickly. When Jesus-followers start living out the life of fullness we are called to; when the church cannot help but put its faith into action; when the body of Christ gets up and gets moving; growth happens. The capacity to reach out and see change in a missional community increases as its members push forwards in vision and action, training themselves in habits of sharing their faith, bringing hope, breathing in more of God, breathing out impact upon people's lives. The community grows as we share the life we have in Jesus with people yet to meet him.

BREATH IS INSPIRATION

Another word for inhalation or breathing-in is 'inspiration'. In respiratory system terms this inspiration is about receiving what the body needs from outside itself, from the oxygen in our atmosphere. For living mission as the church, our breathing-in is literally 'inspiration', the need for input, influence, creativity and ideas from outside ourselves, to then fuel action. Our relationship with God supplies our inspiration, whether through scripture which 'is God-breathed', or through prayer, dreams, visions and the prophetic, or through what we see of Jesus in the people around us and our world. God has created an endless supply of resources to shout of his glory that exists beyond our own understanding and ability. The inspiration that sustains us is constantly required from the author of life and keeps us looking up and reaching out. We cannot breathe if we have nothing beyond ourselves to breathe in.

LOVE CHURCH. LOVE STUDENTS. LOVEYOURUNI.

Oxygen is the basis of life, breathing it is essential for us. If there were no oxygen on our planet, there would be no life as we know it. In the same way, sharing the love of God, pointing people towards Jesus with our whole lives is the oxygen of the church. Without mission there is no missional community, there is no life, no heart, no living mission. Jesus embodied and lived mission. He passed his mandate to love the world and draw all people to himself, on to his followers, to be outworked by them. Us. Our oxygen as Jesus' disciples is to share our lives wrapped-up in the living God with anyone and everyone we come into contact with. Without the oxygen of mission, the body is dead.

To energise the body, particularly if it is suffering from fatigue, or if it is weak, broken and hurting, an intake of oxygen heals, restores and revitalises. In the same way, hearing the good news about Jesus; listening to people's stories of God's faithfulness and break-through in their lives; reading the bible's many accounts of God using ordinary humans like us to do extraordinary things for his glory; these are like breathing in pure oxygen. They remind us why we are alive, they empower us, they encourage us not to give up, to lose hope or fall asleep: the story of God brings life, and life in all its fullness. Since this is the case, prepare yourself for the next few pages, because we are going to share some stories of God using and changing the lives of students. Receive it as oxygen. Breathe deeply.

LIVING BREATHING STORIES

ROSIE'S STUDENT LINKUP STORY

Rosie was touched by how the two girls had come to meet her on campus so soon after her arrival. Having signed up to studentlinkup.org, Rosie was one of the many names on the list of freshers turning up to start student life in a new city. She had received a few welcome emails from different churches who had access to the list, but this meeting on campus had been the first offer of a coffee and a personal connection. A student worker and a third year student turned up, bought her a drink and asked Rosie about her course, her housemates and answered questions about the city and its churches. An hour later, Rosie thanked the girls for taking the time to meet her and encourage her. It was really reassuring to have already made friends with another Christian student. Although she said their particular church was "the wrong end of town" for her to consider joining, she was grateful for their effort and commitment in making sure she settled well into uni life.

The following Sunday, much to Rosie's surprise, she found herself going the extra mile to try out the church the girls were from, since she felt much more confident walking into a place where she would already know people. And after all, they had gone the extra mile for her. Three years later, Rosie is a leader within this same church and looking for jobs in the area so she can continue to invest and live in the community she never expected to end up in.

Finding and connecting to other Christians when you turn up alone at uni is like receiving the breath of life. Missional communities ready to reach out and receive freshers can set the culture and establish what the church looks like for the whole year within those first few weeks of term.

Thousands of Christian university-starters link-up to their new university locations and its local churches, through StudentLinkup.org. Before even arriving on campus, freshers are being contacted by and connected to new churches, welcoming them into the adventure of following Jesus at uni as part of a local community. However, making intentional and lasting connections with freshers is not a given. Helping Christians integrate with and commit to a church during their degree years and reaching those thousands of students who would never use StudentLinkup.org or think of church as an option requires creativity. It requires strategic thinking from current students and the local churches who welcome in each new generation.

Making personal contact is absolutely vital to any connection made with a new student, whether it be sending them a personal message rather than a group email as you introduce your church, or asking individuals to meet for coffee and giving time to listen and really get to know them. Since freshers turn up in their masses, personal contact, a sense of being known, remembered and cared-for, speaks volumes of something different and needed. Missional communities are perfect spaces small enough to really know people and be known like family, but in order to make a newcomer feel comfortable in that setting, one on one contact first can make a huge difference.

CONNECTING WITH THE WIDER STUDENT POPULATION

Meeting keen Christian university starters is one thing, but meeting the thousands of freshers who would never walk into a church is another matter entirely. This is where loving your university really comes into play, being hands-on as a community in serving and welcoming students to your city and campuses.

ANDREW'S FRESHER'S WEEK STORY

Alongside the Christian groups on campus we arranged a 24-7 prayer week during fresher's week, in a tent! We were situated right in the centre of campus so that it was fairly difficult to miss us, with the aim of putting God on the radar of all the students, not just the Christian ones. We had dozens of students pop in to find out what the tent was all about, many asked questions about faith and had prayer requests. We also met many Christians who had drifted away from faith and felt the need to connect back in. By the end of the week people were asking if the tent could be there all the time!

DARREN'S BAG ANGELS STORY

As one of the local churches in our university town, we decided to help freshers move into their halls of residence each year. It's been a great way to meet lots of freshers and serve them and the whole university. To make things more interesting, we created the theme of 'Bag Angels' for the project, dressing up in white boiler suits with painted wings on the back with the words 'Bag Angels' so people could spot us. We hung around in the car parks helping parents and students move in. We got a great response from everyone, we had loads of fun doing it too and it really helped build relationships with the student union and hall committees, which then continued throughout the year.

MIRIAM'S COLLEGE REPS STORY

At the start of my second year, I signed up to be a 'rep' for the freshers arriving at my college. Some universities call this welcoming role 'mums and dads', 'big brothers/ sisters', 'buddies' or something similar. The point is for older students to welcome the new arrivals and take them on their first nights out and try to help the new housemates bond as a group. This role is an ideal one for Christian students to sign up for as you can use the position of leadership and responsibility given to you to genuinely love, encourage and connect with often nervous and unsure freshers. It was through being a college-rep that I saw three of the freshers I met in those first days come along to an Alpha course and get invited into my church community.

Another access point during the first weeks of term can be at freshers' fairs which are often accessible for local churches to have a stand to meet and connect with more students. Some universities welcome a 'churches together' stand, others give individual churches a space when asked. The key is to think through your first point of contact if you are at freshers' fair, because they are often very busy, noisy and totally consumer orientated. Having the right people on your stand, who are energised by meeting new people, good at striking up rapport quickly, and who can get names and numbers for that all important personal follow-up, will make a huge difference.

Fresher's week is full of potential and a chance to set the tone of your student work and your campus' experience of Jesus. If the first weeks of term were a springboard for how you lived out student mission all year, what could this look like? For example, given that every university needs to meet student welfare standards, why not ask your Student Union what you, as the local church, can do to serve and help, beyond fresher events? What are the needs you see on campus that the local church could fulfill? It is these sorts of questions that provoke creative mission responses, such as the stories below.

JAMES'S BIKE STORY

After a bunch of churches in Oxford met together to be encouraged and inspired by how they could love their uni, one student shared how he took action: "Me and some guys started up a free bike fixing station by one of the libraries. One interaction in particular stands out. I was fixing this girl's bike. Like many of the student's bikes in Oxford, it was a death trap. She just kept asking, "Why are you doing this? Do I need to pay you?" I just said, "You know what, Christians seem to be known more for what they stand against than what the stand for. We wanted to do a little bit to change that. We wanted to fix your bike because we believe there is a God who loves you, who loves everyone, and fixing your brakes is just a little way to show some of that love in a practical way." She was really interested in finding out more so I passed on the details about some local churches in the area and where we meet.

TIM'S COMPUTER CLINIC STORY

After being inspired by what it could mean to loveyouruni, Tim from Swansea decided to put his idea into practice: "I study Computer Science and some of my friends and I thought about starting a free 'clinic' where people could come and get their computers fixed for free. I thought it would be a great way to show people Jesus' love using the skills and interests I have and maybe start some conversations. Loveyouruni was really encouraging for me and I'm going to speak to the societies co-ordinator on campus to see if we can get a room or space to start doing some clinics. I even got the idea to dress up as doctors to advertise it!" Not long after, we received this e-mail: "Heeey, Just wanted to let you know that a PC clinic is actually starting in Swansea. We have great backing from the Student Union and we are hopefully going to do it in the students union bar/cafe!!! Praise the Lord!"

COMMUNITY AND MISSION

Community is mission and mission is community. Almost all of the student mission ideas, stories and strategies in this book are actually about community: inviting friends into community; building community with those yet to know

Jesus; finding ways to shine light into the community that exists on campus and in student houses. Some people are more naturally gifted or confident in living a life that builds community than others. It is useful to share stories of ways students can be in community, create it with their housemates and friends and can see people meet Jesus through the family that is the body of Christ.

Up and down the country there are countless stories of normal friendships being built and students coming to know Jesus, simply by living life alongside one of his followers. Just like Jesus shared life with twelve friends, who then recognised him as their Messiah, so our everyday friendships become the heart of missional community and the natural effortless breath of life.

ASHLEY'S DARTBOARD STORY

"Do you believe there is a God?" Was the question asked by James my housemate. We'd had a few beers and had been throwing darts at a dartboard for almost two hours determined to hit treble twenty before going to bed. I thought about it for a bit and James asked again "Would you believe in God if I hit a treble twenty on my next shot?" I thought about it, and he threw.... the dart flew in!! "It's got to be a fluke" I said. "Try again?" ...straight in! "How about a third?" ...Bingo!! This was kind of where it began for me.

"At school and at uni I have always been amazed by science, although, deep down, I have always felt frustrated by my lack of answers. Through finding God I feel satisfied, even relieved that there is an answer. Getting to know God has also allowed me to appreciate his creation more, even when it's not the sunniest of days! Another great fringe benefit of finding God is the superb set of people I have met through church, Alpha, the foundation course I went on and cell. I only wish I had met them all sooner! Knowing God has given me confidence to open up the bible, a book which I have always wanted to pick up, but never been sure if I would understand it. But I think the biggest thing for me in terms of how God has made a difference to my life is the confidence in knowing that I really do have someone looking out for me. It's almost like a weight has been lifted from my shoulders.

Right now at the end of my uni career with no job lined up I am working on keeping the faith, and knowing that the big man will keep me on track and show me where I need to be. Thanks to all you guys that have helped me begin this journey, and thank you God."

IAN'S ULTIMATE FRISBEE STORY

"In all honesty my life before I met God was pretty good, although I always knew there was more out there which I could feel but couldn't quite get my head around. I came to God through a friend called Hannah I met on the Ultimate Frisbee team at university. She was the first Christian I had ever met and I was curious so I fired loads and loads of questions at her; questions about sex before marriage, drink and why she believed in Jesus. It all made some sense, so I decided I would say I was a Christian although I didn't really believe it.

After the Christmas break I began attending Hannah's church. One thing scared me though, people were singing and jumping about as well as raising their hands in the air in jubilation to God. I didn't really get it until the third time I came to a gathering. The singing started, the arms went up, and I felt a hugely overwhelming feeling rush through me, the tears flowed and then I knew that I had met God. Finding a real relationship with God has made me want to be a better person, to live life as it was intended and use my gifts and talents to make the world a better place. It's very exciting."

COME DINE WITH ME

As you journey with your friends, a simple idea to focus the time with your housemates, course mates, team mates or cell can help create depth to your friendships. An example is 'come dine with me' nights where week by week (or whatever your diaries manage) a group of friends take it in turns to host a fancy and fun dinner party at their house. Teaming up with a couple of friends from church and a few of their mates may end up creating a group almost like a cell group/small group. Establishing a regular meet-up around good food and good conversation deepens friendships beyond snatched catch-ups between lectures or on the football pitch. It also lends itself as a format for introducing Student Alpha, or church small group/cell meetings as another thing to build friendships around. And of course, introducing friends who don't know Jesus to friends who do and vice versa just makes sense when building community and pointing people to Jesus.

When community is being created with those that don't yet know Jesus and those who do, questions and discussions about God are likely to arise. This can be a brilliant, fun and a learning experience, but sometimes it can feel challenging and maybe even be avoided for fear of getting 'hard' questions we can't answer. Explaining how humanity fits into the story of God, and fielding discussions about the reason for life, the point of the church, why the world appears how it is and how to encounter this God we believe in, can leave us feeling stuck or inadequate. Student Alpha exists as a tool to help equip us to share our faith with our friends, and create a space and route for us to do just that.

JOSH AND NAOMI'S CELL ALPHA STORY

Josh and Naomi were leading a student cell group in their church and decided to run a Student Alpha course for a term. The course is compressed into seven weeks in order to fit any uni term, and it's free to run, you can simply watch the pre-recorded talks online or present them yourself using all the downloadable scripts and material to help you. Since so many of Josh and Naomi's cell members were in brilliant friendships with students yet to know Jesus, Student Alpha was a helpful tool to carry on building what was already naturally happening in the community. The cell group members all committed to bringing friends along, and hosting it in their homes. There were around twenty-five students a week journeying together in discussing and exploring Jesus. When there were 'too many' Christians in the room, some would leave and wash-up, chat and pray in a next door room to allow their mates plenty of opportunity to speak and not feel in a minority.

GAVIN'S HOUSEMATES ALPHA STORY

Second year student Gavin ran a Student Alpha course, along with myself and another friend, in one of our uni houses for thirteen of our housemates. As a friendship group finding ourselves no longer living together in halls, we wanted to try and meet up and eat together at least once a week, so Alpha complemented the natural community we were building as friends with very little extra work. It allowed our whole friendship group to hear about what we live our lives for and to discuss it with each other. We also had the freedom to disagree or question things, as the talks were pre-recorded so it wasn't as if the speaker was present to get offended! We even did 'the Holy Spirit weekend' one Saturday in town with a couple of friends in their late twenties from our church as guest speakers. We all went out for a meal together, we talked and prayed about the Holy Spirit, and some of our friends encountered the power of God for themselves.

JACKO'S HOMELESS ALPHA STORY

Although its primary aim is to reach far more people through smaller groups in homes and halls, Student Alpha is also used to run bigger-scale centralised courses. Sometimes churches have partnered together to run a course or maybe do a city-wide one in a bar or pub or on campus. In York we have run a couple of centralised Student Alphas as well. During our first attempt at a larger course, we ended up having a discussion group of homeless guys each week who would join us from the street for the evening. Soon, everyone at Alpha became disappointed if our slightly rowdy, but usually pretty funny, homeless guests didn't turn up. They were as much a part of students coming to meet Jesus as the course itself. Both the homeless and the students came to church as a natural part of feeling so involved in the community already, thanks to the weekly gathering.

INTENTIONAL NIGHTS OUT

Some of us love going on nights out, dancing hard until the early hours and dressing up to impress. Others will really struggle to engage in the party-culture of university and want to run for the hills at the thought of being around the drunken escapades and fancy dress themes of student nights. There's no ignoring this side to university life and there are ways we can enjoy being in this world but not of it.

Sometimes all that is needed when you are going on a night out with your mates is to ask a friend to keep you accountable to not drinking more than a pre-agreed amount. This is a simple way to help yourself remain in control and do the best you can in representing Jesus on the dance floor. For others, organising a night out so that you are deliberately going with some Christian mates as well makes a night much more enjoyable. Then you know you're part of a team who are intentionally out to worship God, stay sober and be the joy-bringers to their friends.

Even if it feels like the biggest effort in the world to join your friends at a club, changing your mindset towards a night out so that it becomes an adventure with Jesus can radically change your attitude. You could pray beforehand, have friends praying for you whilst you're out, and keep your eyes open for opportunities to love your mates throughout the night. Yes! The church should be the best party-throwers out there, since we have the most to celebrate, but we also want to go where the masses gather and shine light into those places. Go armed (Ephesians 6), go intentionally, go with the power of God and get ready for the stories that will come out of loving your mates on the dance floor. Use your community to support you, they are there for you as well as to reach your mates.

ANNA'S CLUB MISSION STORY

If you've ever been in a student club on a night out, you will know that the toilets are one of the messiest places to be. This story starts in the girls' toilets. This is a place where tears and arguments, mascara-streaked faces and vomiting in cubicles are commonplace. This is a place where a student and Jesus-follower called Anna from Open Heaven Church decided to hang out and serve the girls she met in distress. Anna, and the team who quickly formed around her, breathed life into the Students' Union simply by helping the girls at their most vulnerable, taking care of them, handing out tissues, chatting and, where appropriate, praying... loving their uni.

This kind of breath of life doesn't go unnoticed. From these early days of simple serving, Loughborough Students' Union have partnered with Open Heaven to create 'Club Mission', the branded team from the church who take care of the pastoral needs of the students every Friday night at the SU events. Club Mission has a chill-out room to which students find their way, knowing that Christians are there to listen to them, chat about life and pray with them, give them a free bottle of water and even walk them home if it's obvious they're never going to make it by themselves. It's also now widely acknowledged that your night out isn't complete without a picture with 'Harry the elephant', the Club Mission mascot! There's also a prayer room constantly manned during the night, and Club Missioners do rounds of the dance floor, helping those in need and working with the bouncers to support the night's safety.

But the story doesn't end there. The biggest SU night of each term is when the weekly Friday Night Disco (FND), is co-branded with Club Mission. The team go all-out on these nights, providing queue entertainment, hot drinks, water bottles, flip flops to help girls in heels home and there are videos about the church playing on the club screens. This is more than Anna and her original team could have asked or imagined as they stood in the toilets a few years ago with the girls drunk and upset on the tiles.

The Club Mission team have stories of God-appointments every week: lots of conversations with students who have a church background but have lost their way at uni, follow-up invitations and opportunities to pray for students. And all this with the support of the Student Union. In fact, Club Mission were awarded 'Team of the Year' at the Loughborough Experience Event. These were some of the endorsements written about them from Union staff who nominated them:

"They have created a chill out room in the middle of a busy night club. They have created something to look after people when they are at their most vulnerable, when they have had too much to drink. They do what they do to serve others; instead of going out with their mates on a Friday night they ensure that everyone else is having a great time. They deal with the individuals; they look after Loughborough Students one person at a time. I can't think of any other group of people that are looking to volunteer to serve Loughborough students in this way. And at all times they don't seek any recognition or praise, they just humbly get on with it. Club Mission has honestly stolen the hearts of all venue staff, and are welcomed with open arms into our FND team. We could never repay them for their hard work."

All of that because one girl saw the breath of God, the image of God in the faces of drunk girls but believed God had more for them. One small community of students living outwardly has changed the Loughborough student experience for years to come.

BREATHING OUT SOCIAL ACTION

Fighting for justice; advocating for human rights; raising money and awareness to eradicate poverty; going the extra mile for a cause: these ideas make sense to our generation of students, a generation that is more connected and aware of the global community than ever before. We are a generation that has been brought up being told that we can all be world-changers, and live the dream. Engaging students with social action not only makes sense and takes minimal persuasion (in terms of seeing the value) but it's also a great way for people who don't know Jesus to encounter a loving and just God who cares about social action more than anyone.

Perhaps Christian students need to be more active in joining justice and human rights societies that already exist on campus? Perhaps we need to set them up, if no one is speaking up for those who can't?

JANE'S EMPTY CUPBOARDS STORY

It was through partnering with a local charity called Besom, who seek to help people in poverty in the local area, that a bunch of students had their eyes opened for the first time to the fact that people were living without any furniture or enough food, only two streets from their student houses. That day, a team of students, some of them Christians, some of them not, worked to re-paint and restore the crumbling council property of a single mum and her son. They also dug deep into their pockets and filled the fridge and cupboards with food. The mum's response: "I haven't seen a fridge of food like that for six months." This is Jesus isn't it? This is what the gospel is. Students ended up bringing that family to church. The church community are still involved in their lives today, two years on.

PIPPA AND MIRIAM'S LAST MINUTE BANQUET STORY

One Friday in November the Fusion team had a day like no other. Luke Smith set his colleagues Pippa and I a surprise challenge: to throw a banquet for the people of York in exactly twelve hours. In the book of Luke, chapter 14, Jesus told a parable of a rich man who threw a banquet. Having been rejected by those on his initial guest list, he opened up the invite to anyone and everyone who would come. Pip and I were read this story and literally tasked to do the same: to host a banquet and invite the people of York - the hungry, the homeless and the lonely and anyone else along the way to come and be blessed. We had to gather the team, raise the money, create the food and make the whole event happen at 7.30pm, having been challenged at

7.30am that same day.

There is no denying that the banquet would not have happened had it not been for around thirty students from local churches responding to our plea for help over social media at the start of the day. Heaps of freshers who we barely knew turned out in force to create our cooking team and wait on tables that night. We just delegated the leadership of most tasks to students who stepped up and gave of their money, time and energy all day and all evening.

The result was breath-taking. During the course of the evening we welcomed into the banquet and fed over one hundred guests. Over six hundred pounds was raised and given away to local homeless projects. Students formed a jazz band, served coffee, made food, gave out nearly eight hundred invitations, welcomed guests, collected food donations from local shops and restaurants. They served our twelve-hour mission with total commitment.

The story of the Banquet proved to me how much students can do with so little time, money, or warning. Students are in a life-stage that means they can just drop everything when called on for exceptional action and be available to go the extra mile, staying up until the early hours. We saw students step up into leadership, commit to local church and create missional community, all in the space of twelve hours. If the breath of life results in more missions like the banquet, we will see people encounter Jesus, the Jesus who gave us simple stories that we can live out literally today, in order to see God change lives. http://bit.ly/LastMinuteBanquet

FASTING SLEEP AND OTHER PRAYER MOMENTS

It was a bunch of students who decided that between 10pm Sunday and 5am Monday they would fast sleep and pray for their mates who didn't know Jesus. It was during one of these nights that the idea of using Google Maps to do a virtual prayer-walk around the student club streets emerged.

It was through an impromptu time of praying and listening to God after a dinner party, that thirteen student leaders who had arrived to start the uni year early, ended up commissioned and inspired to welcome and connect into community more freshers than ever before.

It was through gathering as students before Sunday's church meeting to listen to God beforehand that many of us learnt how to hear the Holy Spirit's whisperings for the first time.

It was during an all-night prayer meeting that a group of students had their hearts broken for their friends and their

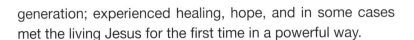

generation; experienced healing, hope, and in some cases met the living Jesus for the first time in a powerful way.

As we breathe in and breathe out, we let the 'oxygen' we feed on, energise, inspire and change us. It flows from the constant dialogue and experience of encountering God in prayer. Prayer changes us, not just the things we are praying about. Changed students, fueled by the Father for mission, change campuses.

NATASHA'S PRAYER AND PROPHECY STORY

Natasha is a student worker who has started gathering small teams of three and four students from her church to head onto campus, praying and asking God to tell them who to meet and what words that person needs to hear to connect with Jesus. One time, the little group had nothing to go on but the picture of a guy in a red hoodie. When they spotted a student in this specific clothing, they took a risk, headed over to him in the canteen and introduced themselves.

They told him they believed in God and that this God loves him. They asked if they could pray for anything for the guy, to which he replied there was nothing and thanked them. So off the team went, feeling like they may have had a 'less successful' encounter but trusting God. This same student then tracked down

Natasha and the team over Facebook, thanking them, as he was in fact a Christian and their message and offer of prayer had prompted a brilliant conversation with his housemates. Subsequently this student has felt called to Natasha's local church where he is now fully involved... all from taking a risk with God on a red hoodie.

As the carriers and bringers of God's breath of life, the words we speak, the prayers we pray, the risks we take, have impact. Listening to God and asking the Holy Spirit to inspire us with words, pictures and insight, to pass on encouragement and point people towards Jesus in love is powerful. When students head out onto the streets and campuses of their cities to meet the people God has prompted them to find, to pass on words of love and encouragement from the Father and to offer prayer freely without any agenda but love, lives are changed.

I remember once when my mate Leon and I began leading 'listening to God' meetings in our college: we would write down any words, pictures and ideas we got as we asked God to point us towards students we could chat to and pray with when we met them after college nights out. Bizarrely, those meetings ended up being massively important in helping us learn how to hear God's voice and gain confidence to take risks in speaking to people about Jesus. We also learnt to be available to meet with specific people in times and places that only God can organise.

ELLIE'S INTERNATIONAL STORY

Ellie was an international student worker at a local church and in her two years in this role saw many Chinese students come to faith. On one occasion, whilst Ellie was chatting to one of her student friends on campus, the student's course mate who had tagged along started flicking through the pages of a Bible the girls had with them. When Ellie looked over, this student was sitting with tears in her eyes looking at the Bible, saying "nobody told me I was made". It was the first time the girl had encountered God, a God who loved her and meant her to be, and it happened without Ellie doing anything apart from being present on campus for these girls.

We cannot underestimate the power in hearing that God exists and loves you and wants to know you, especially to someone who has never ever heard this good news before. It is like receiving the breath of life into a body that is made to breathe but has yet to realise it. For many international students Jesus is a stranger and Christianity is just considered a British tradition as opposed to an ancient truth and foundation of our history.

Reaching out to students who do not speak English as their first language or struggle to engage in UK student culture takes effort. It may be hard to understand them when they speak and require more energy to listen. It will not always be easy to include them in your normal activities as things like trips to the pub are not always comfortable for some cultures. However, as Jesus-followers we have to lead the way in going above and beyond comfort to welcome the strangers and foreigners in our land. Rather than letting the international student in your halls keep themselves to themselves, locked in their room and cooking alone, why not be the one to knock on their door and invite them to eat with you? Why not throw a Sunday lunch for international students to come to and experience a British roast dinner before or after your Sunday church meeting? Yes, some students will come to church in order to experience more of British culture, but we can offer more than that - let us use this openness to be family and love them whilst their own families are so far away.

Jesus tells us to make disciples of all nations, to breathe out his life in all its fullness to the ends of the earth. With overseas students we have an opportunity to do this right on our doorsteps, to share the good news about Jesus to people who can then take it across the world.

SOCIAL MEDIA

Whether we like it or not, social media has created online community in ways that can either speak life and point people towards Jesus, or drain our time, energy and focus away from God. Mastering social media as a tool for connecting with people and building relationship can be a difficult skill. We must pay attention to how we are behaving and what we are communicating online. It is a world with massive impact and influence for the good, the bad and the ugly and everything in-between.

Inviting someone to join an online events page is not the same as asking them in person to come to an event with you. Messaging someone a flyer about the next Alpha course is not the same as inviting them to Alpha and explaining it face to face. Having your religious status set to 'Christian' is not the same as telling your housemates you are a follower of Jesus. Tweeting Bible verses is not the same as putting into practice the words we read from God's book. Texting someone about church is not the same as turning up at their door and walking with them to your mid-week or Sunday gathering.

Our online personas can be helpful at reflecting our lives and values in the flesh, but only if they are reflecting what people know to be true of us when they meet us. When we publish a status about answered prayer and it prompts a course-mate to ask us about faith, then social media proves its worth as a tool to provoke conversation and connection. When we post a blog and a friend we never expected to read it sends us a heart-felt message about their experience and struggles with God, then we realise the value of online platforms. They can start conversations with people who are perhaps not brave enough to begin them face-to-face.

Stop. Pause. Think. When we are tagged in photographs looking worse-for-wear from the night before that we wish hadn't happened, we also need to own the consequences in person. When we are bold about Jesus online and have never actually offered to pray for our friends or tell them about our faith when we're with them, there is a disconnect that leaves a scent of hypocrisy around us. This isn't about living a perfect life with impossible ideals. It is about being wise and consistent. With social media recording our every move, our lives are becoming more and more transparent, so the challenge is to live authentically, online, offline, on a Sunday, on a Monday morning and on a Wednesday night. We want the status of God's faithfulness written all over our faces. How does your online persona reflect and back-up who you are in the flesh, and visa-versa? And how are you using the opportunity of your life on display for the fame of Jesus?

KEEP ON BREATHING

The stories in this book are only a taster of the life and adventures missional communities of students are experiencing right now. The ideas are not exclusive, the students involved are not any more capable of being used by God than you or I. These are stories of the breath of life creating sustainable breathing rhythms from eating together in community or doing nights out in a God-glorifying way, right through to the deep breaths in and out with big Banquet events and Club Mission nights. These are stories to inspire you. The stories remind us that this stuff is possible and is happening in our generation of students. Having a go at reaching out as a missional community of Jesus followers is a joy and a risk. It relies on us being obedient to a faith adventure with God that will take us onto campuses, out of our comfort zones, into the middle of the night and out of this world as we encounter the God of mission, Jesus Christ, who embodied the Father's mission to earth.

LOVING YOUR UNI: 1 CORINTHIANS 13: 3-7 (THE MESSAGE)

Love never gives up.
Love cares more for others than for self.
Love doesn't want what it doesn't have.
Love doesn't strut,
Doesn't have a swelled head,
Doesn't force itself on others,
Isn't always "me first,"
Doesn't fly off the handle,
Doesn't keep score of the sins of others,
Doesn't revel when others grovel,
Takes pleasure in the flowering of truth,
Puts up with anything,
Trusts God always,
Always looks for the best,
Never looks back,
But keeps going to the end.

It's time to begin your own student mission stories. There are so many spheres of influence that your missional community can have in university life. In sports teams, societies, debates, welfare, leadership roles, seminars, theatre, relationships with the local community, influencing the National Union of Students, your lecturers, your housemates, even the modules and subjects you study. All it takes to see the kingdom of God touch earth is a small group of committed followers of Jesus, obedient in reaching out and loving their uni, in the power and grace already given to them. Breathe in. Breathe out.

PART TWO: THE BREATH

PART THREE:

MOVEMENT

WHAT IS MOVEMENT?

"Prophesy to these bones and say to them, 'Dry bones, hear the word of the Lord! This is what the Sovereign Lord says to these bones: I will make breath enter you, and you will come to life. I will attach tendons to you and make flesh come upon you and cover you with skin; I will put breath in you, and you will come to life. Then you will know that I am the Lord.'"
(Ezekiel 37)

We need bones to give us strength and structure. Our bones give our bodies form, they enable us to run, jump and move. They determine our height and our shape and they make us attractive. Without bones there would be no space for the breath to bring life into. God created human beings with the perfect structure to participate in life to the full, to reflect his image and to journey with him.

God's people cannot afford to have student mission structures that are made up of dry bones.

We need our student mission structures to live. We need them to carry life and breath. We need them to know that the Lord is the initiator of mission and God's son is at the centre. It follows then, that how we structure our small group meetings and use that time, either reflects a whole load of dry bones or a living, breathing and attractive community, or something in between!

The final part of this resource draws on some tried and tested structures and pathways that bring life. It focuses on some very practical details that make our missional communities intentional and gatherings that students enjoy being a part of. When God created the world he invested himself into the smallest of details; God then poured himself into humanity. It was perfect. God then gave us free will and there was spontaneity, growth, movement and mess.

Being intentional about how we plan and create the right structures will allow the heartbeat, the values, to be fully expressed. It will allow the breath of God to enter us, and us to carry God's life to others, and it will allow room for spontaneity, growth, movement and mess.

WHAT MAKES A GREAT MEETING?

When we meet together as a small band of disciples of Jesus for 90 minutes each week we want to make the time count. Why settle for another coffee and a chat when transformation and encounter are possibilities? Living mission demands that we raise our game and expectation for gathering together. Great meetings will happen if we give attention to creating the right culture and environment.

CREATING EXPECTATION

Leaders are responsible for communicating the vision and purpose when meeting together and must do so regularly and creatively. This can start with a text or e-mail during the during the day that creates expectation and anticipation before getting together. Once gathered, there needs to be a deliberate shift from spontaneous community time into intentional time. Start by praying or telling a story that will raise faith levels. It might be that you share what you think God wants to do in the meeting or where God is leading this community in the coming months. Make sure everyone feels welcome and that introductions are done each time there is a new face. Clarify again that we 'All Play', everybody's contribution is vital and necessary for community to be built and mission to happen. Sit in an informal 'circle' so everyone can see each other's face and make sure no one is in a place where they could be left out or feel left out. We expect to go deeper with each other and God.

SOME REALLY PRACTICAL STUFF

Meet in a place where you are going to be free to be yourselves before God and that will be easy for people to get to. It sounds cool to meet at the pub but it creates unnecessary distractions and makes prayer and ministry very difficult. So find somewhere comfortable and that won't be too hot or cold (a few student pennies may need to be spent on heating for this time!). Avoid unnecessary interruptions by asking people to turn their mobiles off – we want people to be fully present. Set a time for the meeting to start and try to stick to it. Notice the time as the meeting goes on and encourage people who are contributing to different parts of the meeting to do the same. It is much better to finish on time (no longer than 2 hours) and leave people hungry, than to drag the meeting out.

WHAT DOES GOD WANT TO DO?

Discerning where the meeting is going and what God is doing makes all the difference to your gathering as community. This is a skill all emerging leaders should want to grow and develop. It can be encouraged by looking at three important areas:

1) PREPARATION

This is essential to facilitating a great meeting. Too often meetings seem to have no real purpose or vision because not enough time and effort has been put into preparation. Praying beforehand will give insights into what God wants to say and do when your community is together. It doesn't need to be a protracted time, just long enough to be centred and aware of God. God will often let leaders know ahead of time what he wants to achieve and may even reveal specific things for individuals or the community. Are we available and prepared to work alongside God in the planning of our meetings?

2) THE MEETING

The Holy Spirit will work with the skills and gifting he has given us. It isn't a case of sitting back and 'going with the flow'. Rather, leaders need to be active and alert in recognising what God wants to do, is doing and has finished doing. There is always an element of faith and risk in leading a meeting where the life of God is to be followed and experienced. Knowing how long to stay with a particular section or conversation or prayer ministry, when to move on or when to miss things out altogether will come with practice and having a go.

3) REFLECTION

We learn from our experience, the good and the bad. In order to get the most out of our learning we need to stop and reflect. Our culture doesn't encourage this, always moving on quickly to the next thing. However, developing maturity and lots of new leaders coming through takes time and effort. As leaders become more accomplished, some of this happens quite naturally. For new student leaders, creating a culture and setting an expectation for reflection will help the development both of the individual and the community. This has happened very effectively in gathering the leaders together to meet in 'huddles' and/or regular small group leader training.

LIFE-GIVING STRUCTURES

As a leader or future leader of a missional community any structure you use is there to serve you and to facilitate the life and heartbeat of God. Remember the heartbeat is the sign of life and the breath is the life out-worked, so if the structure feels like dry bones and lacks energy, it is likely it is not facilitating the values. All Christian meetings have a tendency to become dry and dull, but the right structure helps the values to be outworked and gets the heart pounding. My experience is also that where there is little or no structure in small groups there is also little or no discipleship.

One of the most effective structures for student mission I have witnessed in recent decades has been the cell model. I believe it works better in student and campus contexts than anywhere else in society and doesn't require the rest of the church to be doing it. In the early days of Fusion this structure raised up thousands of leaders, encouraged discipleship, was easily reproducible and saw many students find Christ. For reaching the student world it is still a very effective way of structuring missional community.

Cells (or whatever you chose to call them) can be part of clusters, congregations and church plants. They express the raw, the real and the relational elements that are essential for deep and authentic community and mission. They are the day to day 'salt and light', and gathered with the wider church community become 'the city on the hill'. Missional community, in the form of cells, help churches fulfil their God given mandate to reach the universities for Christ. The structure must help us carry out the mandate Jesus gave us (and modelled) for on-going mission and discipleship. In the next section we will explore an effective structure for student focused missional communities.

REFLECT

Running great meetings requires hard work and a number of skills that have to be learned. Consider which areas need to be worked on.

QUESTIONS

- How do you create vision and expectancy for each meeting?
- How confident are you in recognising what God is doing?
- Which of the three areas, Preparation, Meeting or Reflection, do you need to work on?
- What structure do you use that ensures the values are expressed

WHAT HAPPENS WHEN YOU MEET TOGETHER?

INTENTIONAL TIME TOGETHER – A STRUCTURE EXAMPLE

I want to introduce you to a simple structure that helps leaders and members multiply missional communities. The structure includes space for Welcome, Worship, Word and Witness. These four components do not make up a rigid structure, they are simply guidelines to ensure the heartbeat, the values, are all included when the community meets together.

Accomplished leaders may not rely as heavily on the structure. However, if the missional community is effective in seeing new life and attracting new members it will need to multiply or plant a new group. For new leaders having the right structure in place to follow is very helpful and quickly develops confidence.

Whatever structure you use it needs to be
- Easy to understand – it is clear what is being achieved in the meeting.
- Easy to use – others can easily facilitate and pick up the leadership.
- Easy to model – it demonstrates what the community is about.
- Easy to evaluate – it regularly reflects on how the community is doing.

WELCOME

The church should be the most welcoming community on the planet. Thinking about our welcome reminds us we are an inclusive community and all have a part to play. The right welcome refocuses the community on why they are getting together. It creates important space for everyone to participate and contribute. By sharing something about our day, week, relationships, upbringing etc. we facilitate honesty and deepen our appreciation of each other. We feel welcomed and affirmed when we hear others and feel heard ourselves. If we are comfortable with the people in the room, we will be more able to be at ease with God together.

WORSHIP

We know the whole of our lives are worship, but how many times have you rocked up to church or cell group with way too much head noise? So much so that it requires significant effort to even think about worship. If the welcome space allows us to off load in part, some space to centre ourselves on who Jesus is through worship allows us to off load more fully. We have focussed on ourselves and each other, now we focus on God and welcome his presence and agenda. We do this because we recognise Jesus is part of us and at the centre of our community. We want to be fully focused on him.

WORD

The writer of the book Hebrews declares that 'the word of God is alive and active. Sharper than any double-edged sword, it penetrates even to dividing soul and spirit, joints and marrow; it judges the thoughts and attitudes of the heart'. Modelling how this generation can read scripture for themselves and in a small group is absolutely vital. Otherwise people identify themselves as Christians but they never become disciples: media and culture will have influenced them far more than scripture. When we create the space to read scripture it opens up the spiritual adventure of discipleship that is highly energising and deeply challenging. We must read and respond. Study, discussion and sharing should lead to a mix of reflection, repentance and ministry through exercising spiritual gifts and prayer.

WITNESS

Our mission and witness come from valuing people as God values them and a conviction that life with Jesus is a better life. It has to be motivated by love more than duty. As a missional community considerable space needs to be created to think about, plan and pray for our witness. Praying for our friends, prioritising time with them and being accountable in our witness is all part of that. Our witness requires us to live see-through lives in a way that is authentic and at the same time provokes curiosity. Effective mission leads to multiplication and movement. We embrace the growing pains and cost because people are worth it.

REFLECT

Being intentional with our time together means we need some structure. Think about how the heartbeat, the values,

could beat more strongly.

QUESTIONS

- When you assess your meetings, do the values come through the structure?
- Are you able to release and include others in taking responsibility for parts of the meeting?
- Which parts of the meeting do you find easiest and hardest, and why?
- What is the optimum size for meaningful relationships and when do you need to multiply?

HOW DO YOU BUILD COMMUNITY?

Missional communities can and must respond to the ache in student society for real community and for authentic friendships.

'Community' is more than a buzzword, it is foundational to the wellbeing of every human being, yet loneliness is the biggest felt need in our universities today. Through missional community we have a pathway to build and create community in student culture that is inclusive and draws people to Jesus. The values we hold to will define the culture of the community we are building.

Jesus modelled missional community with the twelve disciples. Jesus knew that how he acted would be reproduced in the church as the disciples lived out all that he said and did. He ate, drank and did life with them: the disciples belonged to the group before they fully understood who Jesus was. Jesus prayed for and with his disciples, taught them and modelled community values through his sociable and at times controversial lifestyle. How can we create this kind of dynamic community?

SIX TIPS FOR BUILDING COMMUNITY

1) HAVE FUN

Fun is deeply connected to who we really are. When we experience genuine fun we feel alive and lose our inhibitions – our true self comes to the surface and is free to be and express itself in that moment. Children teach us this truth; it is instinctive and natural to them. Having fun with others is a great community builder. The barriers and inhibitions come down and we often see the best in people.

Most people as they get older become progressively 'unfun'. The Church cannot afford to be a community of such people. The onset of 'unfun' can begin as people enter into adulthood so we need to create, call out and build fun into our relationships. Fun is a part of who we are and it's fun to have fun!

2) SHARE FOOD

Food is a universal language. When we share our food with others we are communicating that they matter, that they have value. When there is a space at our meal table for others we are saying you are welcome here and you are included. When we sit around a table and others participate in eating and drinking with us it is difficult not to strengthen and build a relationship forward.

Sharing food is one of the most effective ways for building community. Don't wait for a birthday or a special occasion, make sharing food a weekly habit, not just with the people you live with, but the people who you want to build with. Sharing food is also fun and it's tasty!

3] ASK QUESTIONS

Questions when directed at us, show us that we have been noticed. Have you ever been in a situation where you have been longing for someone to ask you a question and to take an interest in you? When we ask the right questions of others we start to communicate that we care. Asking the right question is only the start, it also needs to be accompanied by attentive listening. Community gets built as relationships deepen and asking questions provokes honesty, vulnerability and accountability.

Sometimes community gets built to a certain depth and then stops. It is likely asking questions stopped some time ago. Whether we've just met someone or we have been friends for years, asking the right questions builds and keeps community alive.

4] SHOW APPROVAL

Approval is a powerful way of showing that we love a person, it doesn't mean we agree with everything they think, say and do. It is tempting in our culture to flow with the values of mainstream culture in the name of 'inclusion'. Jesus somehow managed a third way. He was deeply, radically inclusive and yet at the same time called people to change. In John chapter 8 he doesn't condemn the adulterous women, he does however ask her to change her behaviour.

People feel strengthened and significant when approved of. If we take a little more time when looking at people we can find many things about them we can approve of and validate. We can begin to see the treasure God has placed in them and speak to who they are becoming in God. We build community as we appreciate people and encourage them.

5) EMBRACE INCONVENIENCE

The road to building community is paved with inconvenience. Fun, food, questions and approval all help act as a counter balance for the cost, sacrifice and the necessity to go out of our way time and again. To create the sort of rugged, robust, loving community we are talking about means that we must learn to embrace inconvenience. And when inconvenience comes knocking on our door, we learn to see it not as an inconvenience, but an opportunity to build community.

6) DO STUFF TOGETHER

Achieving something together is far better than achieving something by yourself. Participating in a common activity or shared task helps people feel part of community and is particularly good for helping men connect. It could be anything from a sponsored challenge to a mission trip, going to a festival together, a local social action project, being bag angels, or to throwing a community banquet.

Doing stuff together not only helps bond the group it also blows away passivity. Missional communities need to be active and engaged with people and causes beyond themselves. Do stuff together, it's also fun!

MISSION

REFLECT

When you consider the community of people you are part of how might you contribute to deepening relationships and growing in authenticity?

QUESTIONS

- How long does it take for people show their true selves? Why is that?
- Who are the best question askers and listeners? What makes them good?
- How does community get built outside of meetings?
- What does inclusivity and inconvenience look like for you?

DISCIPLESHIP PATHWAYS

"I want growth because of salvation, but I equally want growth in maturity because of discipleship. I want to have a deep down satisfaction as I see those belonging to our community actively changing and growing, getting free from the past, getting healed and whole, discovering their passions and gifts and living their lives on purpose. I want a church of life-long learners, students of Jesus Christ, which is what the word disciple means – a learner, student, apprentice."
(Ness Wilson, Team Leader, Open Heaven Church)

The first mention of a disciple is found in Isaiah 8:16 as Isaiah responds to what God has said to him about the future by saying:

"I will write down all these things as a testimony of what the Lord will do. I will entrust it to my disciples, who will pass it down to future generations."

To be a disciple is to be entrusted with God's story.

Disciples are made through a process of discipleship. All Christians need to engage actively in this process for transformation to take place. If we are to build a discipleship culture there are some essential attitudes that need to be modelled by leaders. Those include a willingness and desire to change, a willingness to be confronted and receive from others, a willingness to learn and take responsibility for our own growth.

ONE-TO-ONE DISCIPLESHIP

I believe this is one of the most effective discipleship structures for 18-25 year olds. This model is designed around a relationship where one person is slightly further ahead in their maturity and walk with God. It may be a graduate helping a student, a final year student helping a fresher or a fresher helping a final year student who has recently become a Christian. Jesus modelled intentional and relational discipleship with the disciples and we are let in on a few one-to-one moments with Peter and others.

One-to-one discipleship can't be hurried and needs clear expectations and outcomes that both parties agree to. Here are six areas that anyone who is helping someone else in their discipleship journey needs to think carefully about and be ready to communicate.

1] DISCIPLESHIP IS RELATIONAL

We need to encourage people into whole life discipleship, whether that takes the form of an arm around the shoulder or a kick up backside! If you aren't already, become friends with those who want to grow as disciples and plan occasions where time is spent eating a meal or going out for a drink.

Choose the right people. There may be a God connection or you just like their company or you can easily see their potential. You want to invest in people who are open to God and open to you. Discipleship will work best if they are honest, prepared to change, teachable and hungry to learn. Clear expectations need to be communicated and agreed around the discipling friendship. These include your availability, how often and for how long you meet and when it is time to review the continuation or stopping of this focussed and intentional model of discipleship.

2) DISCIPLESHIP IS HONEST

In order to really help people we need to establish the right to ask questions. This means operating with a 'permission-based authority' that recognises that the only authority we have is the authority that people give us. It is helpful to encourage people to be as clear and defined as possible on this. So permission may be given to speak into their life at any level and ask the difficult questions, or boundaries may be identified for areas that at the present time they do not feel happy talking about. Cultivating a community of people who understand the need for 'see-through lives' allows us the great privilege of journeying with them in areas that really matter. A helpful principle which it might be good for us to verbalise is:

"I won't always be right, but I will be honest with you"

Find out the nature of people's previous experience and understanding of discipleship. Define what it is again using this structure. Also establish if anyone else is helping them on their discipleship journey, maybe in other aspects of their life.

3) DISCIPLESHIP IS REVEALING

The main skill in helping others in one to one discipleship is learning how to ask the right questions. This will become more effective as we journey with more people and grow in discernment. We need to learn to listen on a number of levels. We listen to words that are coming out of people's mouths, we listen to their heart, and from where the words are coming, and we listen to the Holy Spirit. The counsel of the Holy Spirit is available to us and to them.

Asking the right questions uncovers and reveals some of the deep things we fear or are addicted to, as well as where our identity doesn't match up to what God says about us and the hopes, dreams and sense of destiny we carry. Don't be satisfied with superficial answers and accept whatever comes to light. In processing the new awareness that a person encounters never make people's choices for them. Instead explore the options with them, turn to scripture, highlight biblical principles and encourage them to go away and hear God for themselves. Do not cultivate spiritual or emotional dependency, but treat people as adults.

4) DISCIPLESHIP IS STRATEGIC

Fourthly, facilitate a strategy of development for those you are discipling. What things do they need to do or not do, that will help them grow? With God's help identify with them areas of gifting: this is often what they are motivated by and enjoy doing. Together establish a pathway for journeying with a particular area of discipleship. This may mean reading a book, listening to a podcast and/or spending time with a person who has something to offer in that area. Review and reflect on how that pathway serves their discipleship journey.

5) DISCIPLESHIP IS PRAYERFUL

Fifthly, pray for those you are helping in discipleship and seek God for discernment and insight. Learn to watch and observe. Notice what comes to mind or the gut feelings you experience. When you see things in people that need confronting, ask God for the wisdom to know if, when and how to approach them. Remember that God is aware of all our discipleship issues and challenges and has the perfect timing for when to focus on them so that we can grow in greater freedom and wholeness. Any discernment we have and develop in, as we journey with people, needs to be quickly brought to God in prayer: we want to co-operate with God as he works in people's lives. Asking someone to read a particular scripture or to prayerfully reflect on the previous week is often enough for God to give them a new perspective on their life. This allows God to challenge where necessary, rather than it simply being our opinion. And of course pray with the people you are journeying with when you are physically with them as part of your normal rhythm of friendship.

6) DISCIPLESHIP IS REPRODUCIBLE

As we help others on their discipleship journey it is important we aren't laying out advice that we ourselves are not living. We want to be a role-model that people gladly follow and are naturally challenged by. Discipleship isn't about rules and ideals, but about authenticity and aspirations. People need to know they are making progress and so discipleship is about small steps rather than shooting for the moon. We want to raise up faithful followers who will still be running in each decade of their lives. Reproducible discipleship means we are willing to run alongside people for sections of their discipleship journey. All of us need this sort of 'running partner' for discipleship.

Finally and most importantly, love them. Let them know that you really like them and believe in them; take every opportunity to encourage them, affirm them and speak to the very best of who they are becoming.

OUTCOMES OF GOOD DISCIPLESHIP:

1) GREATER SELF-AWARENESS
A recognition of how you come across to others, awareness of strengths and weaknesses, awareness of your defence mechanisms and where you go for comfort.

2) PAIN AND FEAR IS PROCESSED
It has been said that what doesn't transform us we end up transmitting. In Christ our wounds can become sacred and past hurts and fears need not be a barrier to future growth or future relationships.

3) CHARACTER IS DEVELOPED

'God is more concerned with who we are, than what we do and how we do what we do.' We want to help develop a strong sense of identity in Christ both in ourselves and others, so that they know they are valuable, significant and important as children of God before any role or function. Real discipleship is about transformation on the inside, not copying behaviour.

4) GIFTING IS DEVELOPED

Spiritual gifting is released and affirmed so that the good news of the Kingdom is proclaimed and demonstrated in every person's life. The church is strengthened and built up through the gift and contribution of each member.

5) DELIBERATE GROWTH

Discipleship requires conscious and deliberate action, or it doesn't happen, each of us has to choose to enter into a learning and change journey. Setting obtainable goals in place will help vision and dreams become reality. Creating a 'road map' for where we, and those we are on the discipleship journey with want to go, allows us to take a step at a time and track the progress.

6) DECISION MAKING HAPPENS

We need to take responsibility for the decisions we have made and will make. It has been said 'that the quality of our daily life depends upon the quality of our daily choices'. We learn how to make wise and godly choices, using biblical principles, common sense and accountability.

7) SIN CONFESSED

As patterns of sin are overcome, we become increasingly quick to repent, we refuse to come under condemnation and we use accountability to safeguard ourselves. We persevere until new habits and behaviour feel just as comfortable as the old ones and we learn how to respond rather than react to situations, developing greater self-control of emotions.

8) CHURCH COMMITMENT

Discipleship produces a high view of God and a high view of God's people. A commitment to church is really a commitment to people and must go beyond worship style, personal preference and consumerism. A commitment to church means building healthy relationships and being rooted into the community of God's people.

In the heart of most leaders is the desire to build things of eternal value. The best way to ensure that what we have invested our lives in carries on well after we have gone, is to build with people.

An old African proverb that carries much wisdom says:

"If you're going to build for a year, plant grain.
If you're going to build for a decade, plant trees.
If you're going to build for a century, plant people."

DISCIPLESHIP HUDDLE

Another pathway for discipleship that works especially well for leaders is a 'Huddle'. A Huddle is a discipleship structure for current or future leaders that provides support, challenge, training and accountability. Huddles have 4-8 people in them and the participants are invited into a discipling relationship by the Huddle leader.

The purpose of Huddle is to provide a regular time for this group of current or future leaders to be invested in, held accountable for their own discipleship and trained so they can then go and do the same for others. People in a Huddle are expected at some point in the journey to lead a group of their own and build a discipleship culture within it. That might mean starting a Huddle of their own, or it could mean leading a small group or missional community.

There are a few things that uniquely characterize Huddle:

1) TWO QUESTIONS

At the conclusion of each Huddle each participant will be able to answer these two questions: What is God saying to me and what am I going to do about it? These are the two fundamental questions of Christian spirituality that Jesus lays out in the parable of the wise and foolish builders at the end of the Sermon on the Mount.

2) ACCOUNTABILITY

At the beginning of the next Huddle, each participant will be asked how their plan went. Rather than a view of accountability that looks like spiritual policing, Huddle is a place of spiritual partnership.

3) LANGUAGE

A Huddle is a place where the group will learn a common discipleship language that will not only help shape their life, but that they can also pass on to others.

4) LEADER

A Huddle is a place where the leader is offering their life as something to be examined for how Jesus is actively working in it. They are certainly not a perfect example, but they can serve as a living one.

5) REPRODUCTION

An expectation that at some point, each participant will begin leading a discipling community of their own.

HUDDLE DISCIPLESHIP QUESTIONS

CHARACTER UP	CHARACTER IN	CHARACTER OUT
Do I make enough space for prayer?	Do I love the church?	Do I have a heart for the lost?
Do I pursue intimacy with Jesus?	Is time a blessing or a curse?	How often do I share my faith?
What is on my heart for intercession?	Am I resting enough?	Do I leave time for relationships
Am I living in the power of the Spirit?	How are my relationships with my friends?	with non-Christians?
Am I seeing personal revival?	Am I experiencing intimacy in relationships?	Am I running the race with perseverance?
Do I still feel pleasure?		Do I have a vision?
Am I living in a state of peace?	Do I keep my promises?	Am I dying to success?
Am I afraid or nervous?	How easy it for me to trust people?	Am I proud of the Gospel or ashamed?
Am I obedient to God's prompting?	Am I helping other others in their discipleship?	Am I a servant?
	Is my family happy?	Do I find it easy to recognise people of peace?
	Am I sleeping /eating well?	Can I take risks?
	Am I making myself vulnerable to others?	

SKILLS UP	SKILLS IN	SKILLS OUT
Is the worship in my group dynamic and full of intimacy?	Do members of my group feel cared for?	Is my group growing?
Do I find it easy to receive guidance for the next step in the life of my group?	Am I effective at resolving conflict?	Am I too controlling as a leader?
How easy is it to talk to a whole group from 'the front'?	Do I take on the discipline of confrontation?	How welcoming is my group to new people?
Can I teach effectively from God's word?	Is my group living as a community?	Can all group members identify at least one 'person of peace'?
Does my group share the vision God has given me?	Have I defined my own boundaries well?	Am I using leaders in my group effectively?
Do I feel relaxed about leading times of Holy Spirit ministry?	Am I flexible?	Do I find it easy to multiply groups?
	How are my weaknesses as a leader compensated for by others?	Are those I am discipling turning into effective leaders?
	How do I cope with overly dependant people?	Is my group effective in regularly doing 'out' activities?
	How do I cope with controlling group members?	Does my group have a single 'people group' in mind?
	Are there difficulties in my relationships with co-leaders/assistant leaders?	

See www.3dmuk.com for more information, explanation and resources for Huddles and missional communities.

REFLECT

Think about the people around you who you can help on their discipleship journey. What has that help looked like so far?

QUESTIONS

- Who are you looking to for discipleship help and who should you be helping?
- Which are the main outcomes of discipleship that you need to work on?
- What would starting or being part of a Huddle look like for you?
- Which of the Huddle discipleship questions do you need to ask at the moment?

THE END OF THE BOOK AND THE START OF THE MOVEMENT

THE END OF THE BOOK AND THE START OF THE MOVEMENT

As Rich and I sat with mugs of tea, piecing together this book, chewing through what should and shouldn't make the final cut, we had a simple, focused goal. Within these pages, we prayed that students would have enough tools, encouragement and boldness to intentionally live their university days following Jesus and sharing him with those around them.

Imagine if every Christian student deliberately used university as a time to grow up to be more like Jesus, to be challenged and released, shoulder to shoulder with church family members. Imagine if every person who reads this commits to doing life in community with other brothers and sisters, in relentless pursuit of the goal of facing outwards together to share the good news about Jesus. We have the heartbeat of the gospel, causing the breath of life as the body engages in activity and movement, causing yet more breath, a stronger heartbeat, more life, new life, saved lives. The overflow effect of the love of God, the heartbeat of missional communities, is life and more life.

If we all decided to live in missional community in and around our university campuses and cities, I believe we would see these places transformed by every-day, normal, radicals known as Jesus-followers. We would see moments of students reflecting God's love to their mates snowball into a movement of student mission across the nations.

That is the prayer. That is the hope. That is what I see in the growth of the early church recorded in the Bible. So why not again? Why not in this generation of students? If not us then who? If not now, then when?

Romans 10. 14-15 says this:

> *'How, then, can they call on the one they have not believed in? And how can they believe in the one of whom they have not heard? And how can they hear without someone preaching to them? And how can anyone preach unless they are sent? As it is written: "How beautiful are the feet of those who bring good news!"' (TNIV)*

The Message translation of the Bible puts it like this:

> *'But how can people call for help if they don't know who to trust? And how can they know who to trust if they haven't heard of the One who can be trusted? And how can they hear if nobody tells them? And how is anyone going to tell them, unless someone is sent to do it? That's why scripture exclaims,*
>
> *"A sight to take your breath away!*
> *Grand processions of people*
> *telling all the good things of God!"'*

Let us be a sight to take the breath of the world away. Let the Jesus-following students of this land be like a grand procession of people through our university landscapes, building community and walking in the power of God with every step. May our mates come to know their maker for themselves because we were faithful.

Just as Paul asks how people are expected to hear about Jesus unless someone is sent to go and share the good news, consider this your commissioning. We pray this book becomes part of your sending-out, a spring-board into the living, breathing adventure of student mission. We believe students can be spectacular because we have a spectacular God who lives in us. Live, breathe, move forwards with Jesus, we await more stories, your stories, from the movement we are all joining.

The Start.

THE END OF THE BOOK AND THE START OF THE MOVEMENT

ABOUT
FUSION

ABOUT FUSION

Over the next 25 years one billion students will go through the world's universities and colleges.

For a short time, some of the brightest minds gather together in their most formative years. Students from every nation, studying in every nation. Universities and colleges are greenhouses where the seeds of potential begin to germinate. They eventually grow to become world leaders, church leaders, business leaders, teachers, doctors, scientists, lawyers, entrepreneurs, inventors, philanthropists, politicians, producers, authors, actors, artists, musicians…

They will shape the future and shake the culture.

What if in every university city in the world a local church had welcomed them?

What if a local church had reached out to them?

What if a local church had invited and released them into Kingdom life with Christ?

Would the world change?

We think so.

ABOUT FUSION

Fusion is passionate about student mission and is committed to fuelling the fires of a global student movement through:

EQUIPPING STUDENTS:

Inspiring evangelism, resourcing discipleship and preparing new students for university

SERVING CHURCHES:

Connecting students to church, catalysing mission and strengthening church-based student work

DEVELOPING STUDENT WORKERS:

Training, resourcing and encouraging all those in student ministry

Fusion is about connecting student to church and church to student. Not just one or two but serving thousands of churches in reaching and discipling millions of students. We are convinced that local church needs to be at the heart of student mission and students at the heart of local church. We invite you to partner with us in bringing God's love to the universities, see this generation respond to Jesus and make a difference with their lives.

[fusion]

CHURCH PARTNERSHIPS AND CHURCH PLANTING

CHURCH PARTNERSHIPS AND CHURCH PLANTING

Fusion partner with over 750 churches in the UK and a growing number internationally. Fusion also partner with church networks, these include Elim, Groundlevel, New Wine, Pioneer, Salt & Light and Vineyard. They all share our passion for students and have opportunities for students to be involved in missional communities and church plants. Pioneer helped sponsor this book and has some unique opportunities for students.

ABOUT PIONEER

Pioneer is a UK based movement of churches and ministries. Alongside others, we are committed to the re-evangelisation of our nation and to see the Kingdom of God expressed in every sphere of society and culture. We believe that the local church is the primary, though not exclusive, agent of the Kingdom of God and our vision is to see strong, diverse and healthy churches planted and existing churches resourced and growing.

As Pioneer we have many church planting opportunities in different parts of the UK for students to get involved in. We want to release this generation of students into leadership. If that is something that excites you please get in touch. admin@pioneer.org.uk